D0207831

A SEASON TO REMEMBER

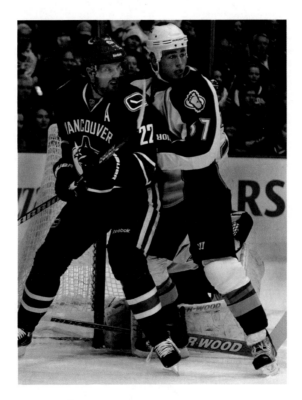

The VANCOUVER CANUCKS' *Incredible* 40TH YEAR

A SEASON TO REMEMBER

GRANT KERR

HARBOUR PUBLISHING

For the real fans of the Vancouver Canucks, who remain loyal and supportive, even after such a heartbreaking finish to the longest season. They are the true supporters of a franchise that has brought so much joy to the sports culture of the West Coast.

Text copyright © 2011 Grant Kerr
Photographs © Pacific Newspaper Group (PNG)

2 3 4 5 — 15 14 13 12 11

All rights reserved. No part of this publication may be reproduced, stored in a retrieval system or transmitted, in any form or by any means, without prior permission of the publisher or, in the case of photocopying or other reprographic copying, a licence from Access Copyright, www.accesscopyright.ca, 1-800-893-5777, info@accesscopyright.ca.

Harbour Publishing Co. Ltd.
P.O. Box 219, Madeira Park, BC, V0N 2H0
www.harbourpublishing.com

Cover, bottom: Ryan Kesler (arms up) and Mason Raymond celebrate a second overtime goal against the San Jose Sharks, May 24 2011 (Ian Lindsay/PNG). Cover, top and opposite: Fans celebrate the third Canuck goal of the first period against the Dallas Stars at Rogers Arena, January 24, 2011 (Stuart Davis/PNG). Cover, back: Canucks win over Chicago Blackhawks, Game 7, Western Conference quarter finals, April 26, 2011 (Gerry Kahrmann/PMG). Page 1: Daniel Sedin battles Colorado Avalanche, November 24, 2010 (Steve Bosch/PNG). Page 2–3: An estimated 150,000 Canucks fans poured into Vancouver's downtown core to watch Game 7 of the 2011 Stanley Cup finals on big screens (Jason Payne/PNG).

Edited by Silas White
Cover design by Anna Comfort O'Keeffe
Text design by Mary White
Printed and bound in Canada

| Canada Council for the Arts | Conseil des Arts du Canada | BRITISH COLUMBIA ARTS COUNCIL An agency of the Province of British Columbia |

Harbour Publishing acknowledges financial support from the Government of Canada through the Canada Book Fund and the Canada Council for the Arts, and from the Province of British Columbia through the BC Arts Council and the Book Publishing Tax Credit.

Library and Archives Canada Cataloguing in Publication

Kerr, Grant
    A season to remember : the Vancouver Canucks' incredible 40th year / Grant Kerr ; introduction by Greg Douglas.
Includes index.
ISBN 978-1-55017-564-6
    1. Vancouver Canucks (Hockey team)—History. I. Title.
GV848.V35K47 2011   796.962'640971133   C2011-906513-4

Contents

The hit everyone was waiting for—Vancouver's Dan Hamhuis
upends Boston's Milan Lucic in Game 1 of the Stanley Cup final in
Vancouver. Lucic skated away. Hamhuis didn't. IAN LINDSAY/PNG

FOREWORD

My, how times have changed. When Vancouver and Buffalo entered the NHL in 1970 as expansion franchises, hockey fans throughout British Columbia were so enthralled about being part of the action that wins or losses didn't seem to matter.

The focus in those infant years was on the opposition. Just to be able to watch live and in person the likes of Gordie Howe, Bobby Hull, Guy Lafleur, Brad Park, Bobby Orr and Darryl Sittler kept the paying customers at Pacific Coliseum satisfied.

It seemed not to faze them that the Canucks finished sixth in the East Division in 1970–71 and seventh in the ensuing three years. The win column over those four 78-game seasons read 24, 20, 22 and 24.

"It was a tough grind," says Orland Kurtenbach, who captained all four of those struggling teams. "Sure, it would have been great to win more games for the fans in those early years. But they stood by us through thick and thin."

Finally, in 1974–75, the Coliseum faithful got their first taste of success when goaltender Gary (Suitcase) Smith suddenly emerged with a stellar season that resulted in the Canucks winning the Smythe Division with 38 wins and 10 ties in an 80-game schedule. Smith was in the nets for 32 of those victories, leading Vancouver into its first ever playoff series.

The Canucks fell 4–1 in games to the mighty Montreal Canadiens and suddenly the pressure mounted on management once fans on the west coast got a taste of post-season play.

And it's been that way ever since. Twice now in Vancouver's franchise history the Canucks have come within one game of winning the Stanley Cup championship and both times hockey journalist Grant Kerr has joined the journey every step of the way. The seventh game losses in New York in 1994 and at home to Boston this past year have merely wetted the appetites of those anxious and loyal Vancouver supporters.

It should be pointed out that Kerr's knowledge of the game goes beyond observing proceedings from the press box. He also has an extensive background as an amateur hockey coach and was acknowledged by the BC Hockey Benevolent Association in 2001 as the 15th recipient of the prestigious Jake Milford Plaque. The award is reserved for "persons whose contributions to hockey in British Columbia have been significant, of lasting impact and generally above and beyond the call of duty."

Kerr was also inducted into the BC Hockey Hall of Fame in 2009.

These honours are noted here to emphasize the value of the author's analytical approach to the intricacies behind the mission faced by Canucks' president and GM Mike Gillis and his management staff during the 2010–11 NHL season.

Advancing to the seventh game of a Stanley Cup Final doesn't come easily. It is the classic example of enduring blood, sweat and tears.

"So close they came to claiming the Stanley Cup," Kerr writes, "but eventual heartbreak when the Canucks couldn't finish the assignment when they were just a single game from immortality."

Indeed, it would have been cause for colossal celebration had the Canucks captured hockey's revered silver chalice in the team's 40th year of existence.

It was an electrifying effort ... one you can enjoy to the fullest in the following pages.

—Greg Douglas, 2011

Roberto Luongo returned to top form in 2010–11, posting 38 wins with a goals-against average of 2.11 and a .928 save percentage. He and backup Cory Schneider won the Jennings Trophy for allowing the fewest goals. RIC ERNST/PNG

## CHAPTER ONE

"We've spent a lot of time trying to remove the negativity around this team. That's a challenge that has been remarkable in my tenure."
—Mike Gillis at mid-season

In the beginning

The saga of what turned into a remarkable season began after the Vancouver Canucks were eliminated from the 2010 playoffs by an aggressive Chicago team in six games. The Blackhawks went on to claim their first Stanley Cup in forty-nine years, while Vancouver management regrouped following a final 5–1 loss. The Canucks had been pushed around by the Blackhawks in no uncertain terms. Chicago made life miserable in the crease area for goalkeeper Roberto Luongo. Plus, the Blackhawks took great delight in pushing around the more timid, albeit skilled, Canuck forwards like the talented Sedin twins, Henrik and Daniel.

Canucks president and general manager Mike Gillis and his staff are haunted by how the team had been beaten two straight years by Chicago in the second round of the post-season. The Canucks appear to have enough skill to be successful, but do they have the grit and determination for the long haul of four playoff rounds? That question is posed over and over to staff members, with Gillis consulting with his trusted confidants, sage hockey men like vice-president of player personnel and assistant GM Lorne Henning, vice-president of hockey operations and assistant GM Laurence Gilman and senior advisor to the GM Stan Smyl, along with head coach

Canucks GM Mike Gillis right, with former Canucks captain Markus Naslund, displayed a sure touch in his third year at the helm, earning the NHL's GM of the Year Award. RIC ERNST/PNG

Alain Vigneault. What kind of team do they need to be successful?

In Gillis's two years as Vancouver GM—it's his first NHL appointment after playing in the league for several years with Colorado and Boston, going to law school and working as a player agent for over fifteen years—he has tried to change the culture of the Canucks through thinking outside the box. He encourages monitoring players' eating habits and sleeping regimens. Gillis constantly plays his cards close to the vest, leading some observers to feel he's on the standoffish side. No matter your opinion of the man, you have to give him credit for doing due diligence to pursue his goals.

The Canucks amassed 103 points in 2009–10, won the Northwest Division and finished sixth in the Western Conference. Twelve playoff games later, against the Los Angeles Kings and Chicago, they were done and gone from the post-season. Gillis knows he has to reshuffle the deck. Bringing in a greybeard like Mats Sundin, as he did in 2008–09, will not do. Nor could he bring back his former client, forward Pavol Demitra, who was beyond prime time. This time the Canucks need fresh legs and a better sense of what it would take to get by the Chicagos of the NHL. The reloading results in the departures of Willie Mitchell, Demitra, Kyle Wellwood, Steve Bernier, Michael Grabner, Ryan Johnson, Darcy Hordichuk, Andrew Raycroft and (after training camp) Shane O'Brien. Some were fan favourites, others were not. But there can't be sentimentality in a business when the bottom line must be expanded, in this case toward a return to the Stanley Cup final after a seventeen-year absence.

The Canucks have decided that the defence needs to

be more consistent in front of the beleaguered Luongo, a top-notch netminder who tends to become a little too emotional in stressful times. Luongo, going into the first year of a lengthy contract that calls for $10 million US in the coming 2010–11 season, needs to be reassured he'll be defended properly when teams such as Chicago crash the crease. Gillis knows he must placate Luongo because there's another problem that has to be solved later in the summer. He decides Luongo should no longer be captain of the Canucks, feeling Luongo is under enough strain being a goaltender and doesn't need the distractions that go along with the captaincy, namely facing the inquiring media on an almost daily basis.

Management scans the player lists of rival teams and decides to target two players. One is Dan Hamhuis, a British Columbia boy from Smithers who has played six NHL seasons with the Nashville Predators, who made him a first-round draft pick in 2001, selected twelfth overall. Hamhuis is respected league-wide for his steadiness and reliability. He has a calm nature to his play that is attractive to the Canucks. He can hit effectively, especially with bone-jarring hip checks, and his outlet pass from the defensive zone is on-the-tape accurate. Best of all, Hamhuis is about to become an unrestricted free agent. If signed by the Canucks, they would not have to compensate the Predators, a Western Conference rival.

The Canucks also like the style of another defender, Keith Ballard, a rambunctious hitter with the Florida Panthers who apparently has fallen out of favour with the coaching staff. Ballard is an American from small-town Minnesota who has five NHL seasons under his belt with the Phoenix Coyotes and Florida, and also was a first-round pick, taken in 2002 by Buffalo eleventh overall. Ballard and Hamhuis impressed Vancouver's pro scouts with their tenacity in the defensive zone. They would take the body when necessary and believed strongly in looking after business around the net. The Canucks want not just more depth on defence, but personnel that will make life easier on Luongo.

Gillis moves swiftly to get his plan in place. On NHL draft day on June 25, he springs into action. The Canucks acquire Ballard and right winger Victor Oreskovich from the Panthers, with right winger Steve Bernier, left winger Michael Grabner and a first-round draft pick going to Florida. The Canucks get their man at a huge price, considering Grabner will go on to score thirty-four goals with the New York Islanders after being placed on waivers by the Panthers. Florida GM Dale Tallon also got the pick he wanted, using his third selection in the first round to take centre Quinton Howden from Moose Jaw in the Western Hockey League.

Now the Canucks look to add one of the most sought-after defencemen available on the free agent market. Hamhuis is being courted by both the Philadelphia Flyers and the Pittsburgh Penguins. Through his quiet proficiency, he has earned the right to gain financial security in a workplace of his choice. Hamhuis chooses Vancouver on July 1, the first day of free agency 2010. He elects to return to his BC roots, with the Canucks as the benefactors. They add a top-four defender who can hold his own against any of the opposing top lines in the league. Hamhuis signs for six years at an average salary of $4.5 million.

Vancouver ownership headed by the Aquilini Investment Group Inc. has stepped to the plate and hit

a home run. The three Aquilini brothers—Francesco, Roberto and Paolo—support their general manager in the best way they know how. Now the Canucks are knee-deep in expensive and experienced defencemen. In addition to Hamhuis, Ballard will earn $4.2 million a season, Alex Edler $3.25 million, Kevin Bieksa $3.75 million, Sami Salo $3.5 million, Christian Ehrhoff $3.1 million, Andrew Alberts $1.05 million and Aaron Rome $750,000. The defence puzzle piece is in place. Now it is time to address the captaincy.

Gillis flies to Montreal to have a face-to-face conversation with Luongo. The GM, after consultations with his staff and head coach Vigneault, wants Luongo to relinquish the captaincy. It's time for Luongo to concentrate on his positional play, rather than all the distractions that come with representing teammates in the issues that dominate dressing room conversations. Gillis is asking Luongo to swallow his pride and do what's best for the team, in the opinion of management. It's a tough sell, but in the end, Luongo comes to realize that Gillis holds the cards and the goaltender relents. It is mid-summer and the Canucks are without a team captain; that issue will be resolved later during training camp.

Gillis has taken major steps to adjust team chemistry. The defence has been strengthened by veteran players who bring a definite hardness to their game; they should make the Canucks tougher to play against. So should some additions to the forward lines, especially in the bottom six, or grinding positions. It's long

Top-four defender Dan Hamhuis came over from Nashville to upgrade the Canucks' back line. RIC ERNST/PNG

been a belief in NHL circles that players who are not top-six or skilled forwards should be difficult to play against. They should be abrasive in their approach to the game, at least some should be able to kill penalties, and one or two should be willing to stand up for their teammates when the games get rough and out of hand. The Canucks need fortification in these areas. Gillis uses free agency to attract newcomers Manny Malhotra and Raffi Torres, recruited to bolster the third line. Malhotra, a centreman adept at winning faceoffs, especially in the defensive zone, comes from the San Jose Sharks for $2.5 million a year for three seasons. Torres, a rugged left winger with the reputation for delivering heavy body-checks, comes from Buffalo for one year at $1 million.

Beginning his third season as Canucks GM, the calculating Gillis makes significant progress toward icing a team that could move ahead and into the elite of the league, meaning past the second round of playoffs and into the final four. He knows Vancouver fans are fed up with losing to Chicago and he wants his team to be more resilient, to play more like the Detroit Red Wings, where puck possession is more important than banking passes off the glass and out from the defensive zone. Fans paying big bucks at the newly named Rogers Arena want more, much more from their hockey heroes. Gillis also wants his players to be comfortable in handling their emotions when they come up against teams like Chicago, which press the issue through physicality—in most cases directed at Luongo, or the Sedins.

The Canucks add more parts during the summer by also signing free agent forwards Peter Schaefer and Jeff Tambellini. They are intended to provide depth in case of injury, or if other players like promising rookie Cody Hodgson don't meet expectations. Another decision that will prove beneficial is the determination that goaltending prospect Cory Schneider is ready to play in the NHL full-time as Luongo's backup, and that Schneider should get at least twenty starting assignments. The rest would allow Luongo to be better prepared for the playoffs and, hopefully, the long run to the Stanley Cup final. Schneider has been Vancouver property for some time, having been drafted in the first round in 2004 from Boston College. Schneider has performed well in the minors with the Manitoba Moose in the American Hockey League and is considered to be technically sound. He is also open to instruction, important because the Canucks also change their goaltending coach in this off-season.

Gillis replaces Ian Clark with Roland Melanson, which is significant because Melanson sold himself to the Canucks as an instructor who could improve Luongo's positioning in the net. Melanson believes NHL goaltenders should play deep in their goal crease, or in the blue paint, because it lessens the chance they'll get caught up in traffic caused by crease-crashing opponents like Chicago. Melanson has been on the coaching staff of the Montreal Canadiens and worked with Carey Price and Jaroslav Halak, the latter traded to the St. Louis Blues in the summer following a brilliant run in the 2010 playoffs with the Habs. Melanson has twelve years' experience as an NHL goaltender, mostly in a backup role, and a sense of what kind of role the backup plays. The Canucks also bring in another assistant coach when Newell Brown joins the team after leaving the Anaheim Ducks. Brown comes in to work with the Vancouver power play. As a

player he was drafted by Vancouver in 1982 (he never played an NHL game, but was captain of the Canadian national team).

The off-season also sees Gillis and the operations staff decide to honour several former players and coaches during the team's fortieth campaign (the expansion franchise entered the NHL for the 1970–71 season). "The Ring of Honour" is established and four players—Orland Kurtenbach, Kirk McLean, Thomas Gradin and Harold Snepsts—are selected for special pre-game ceremonies that will involve their photos being displayed high above the ice surface. Others are to be introduced before games as the Canucks make a special effort to reach out to the alumni in a "40 Stories-40 Nights" theme. Designated to highlight the celebrations is the raising of Markus Naslund's No. 19 sweater into the rafters to join the No. 16 of Trevor Linden and the No. 12 of Stan Smyl, plus the unveiling of a statue outside the rink of Hall of Fame coach Roger Neilson, who led the Canucks to their first Stanley Cup final in 1982.

Plans are also made to make sure the 1994 Canucks team would not be forgotten for their memorable run to the Stanley Cup final and seven exciting games against the New York Rangers. But at the end of the day, this off-season is all about making sure today's players and fans realize that Gillis and his staff are serious about taking the 2010–11 Canucks to another level. Gillis has stepped up and fortified his roster the best way possible,

Highlight of the 40th-anniversary celebrations was a special night for former team great Markus Naslund, who came back to see his number 19 Jersey retired on December 11. RIC ERNST/PNG

at least in his eyes. The table is set for a season where one of the Canucks marketing slogans would be, *We are all Canucks*.

## CHAPTER TWO

"Other teams are going to want to bring their best games against us. I actually think that will help us. It will challenge us."

—Dan Hamhuis
before the 2010–11 regular season

All the president's men

One of the most creative off-seasons in the forty-year history of the NHL Canucks is about to be put to the test. Will Gillis's moves bolster a Vancouver team apparently capable of moving ahead into the elite of the final four? In a city that craves a championship, getting to the third round and then the Stanley Cup final is all that matters. GM Mike Gillis has done his job and now it's up to head coach Alain Vigneault to take the newest pieces and make sure they mesh with holdovers. The Canucks are picked as a Stanley Cup finalist before the season by EA Sports, the video-game kings. Many journalists and broadcasters have the same feeling, a sense that Vancouver can rise above all else in the West, including the Cup champions in Chicago. The Blackhawks have a much weaker roster after several players were traded due to salary cap restrictions, including most of the grinders that made them the better team against the Canucks.

The Sedin twins in particular feel the team has been strengthened. They like the additions, even though they will start the season without linemate Alex Burrows, who is still rehabbing his shoulder following summer surgery. He has been the best fit at right wing with the Sedins because Burrows can think on the move. Burrows won't overpower anyone with his shot, but he can skate with speed, pass the puck effectively, get to the net and forecheck. Vigneault has at times moved Burrows away from the Sedins, but eventually

Super twins Henrik and Daniel Sedin made NHL history in 2010–11, becoming the first brothers to win the league scoring title on back-to-back years.

GERRY KAHRMANN /PNG

Burrows returns and everything falls into the place for the trio.

During the pre-season, power-play coach Newell Brown likes the work of Ryan Kesler when he puts the No. 2 centreman with the Sedins during man-advantage situations. Kesler is bigger and sturdier than Burrows and has a knack for tipping in goals from point shots. When he returns in November, Burrows will get his power-play time on the second unit. Kesler and Burrows are also effective when used as a pairing in penalty-kill situations. They are fearless when blocking shots and have a knack for clogging passing lanes with their sticks.

Dan Hamhuis has brought stability from his years of experience in Nashville. Hamhuis isn't flashy on the back end, but he plays with an inner confidence that shows his new teammates he is reliable. Soon Hamhuis also shows he can join in the rush, an offensive tactic that associate coach Rick Bowness encourages in attempting to create more odd-man situations in the offensive half of the ice. Eventually Hamhuis will be partnered with veteran Kevin Bieksa, with Bieksa producing some of the best hockey of his career as he plays for a new contract next season. Hamhuis accepts the outlook of Canuck veterans. In Nashville, the team objective was to make the playoffs; Vancouver's objective is to reach the Stanley Cup final and win the team's first Stanley Cup.

In goal, Luongo has come to grips with playing fewer games as he shares more of the workload with rookie Cory Schneider. It's a healthy situation when the incumbent is open to change, especially after Luongo is no longer team captain. That duty falls to Henrik Sedin, the older of the twins by six minutes. Hank, as he's called by brother Daniel, is coming off a season when he won the NHL scoring championship and Hart Trophy as the league's most valuable player. Although there's never any mention publicly, insiders get the feeling Daniel wants to strut his stuff this season, show that he can be every bit as productive as his brother. Henrik produced 112 points last season when he played all eighty-two games in the regular season, averaging 1.37 points a game. Daniel missed nineteen games through injury and managed 85 points, an average of 1.35 a game.

But their objectives for the 2010–11 campaign are the same: they want more playoff success for the team that brought them to the NHL in 2000. The Sedins were drafted second and third overall in the 1999 NHL entry draft after a series of trades by then-general manager Brian Burke to make sure he got to select the teenagers from Örnsköldsvik, Sweden. They are identical in just about every way, except one: Daniel is more a pure goal scorer and Henrik more the playmaker. Through nine NHL seasons, Henrik has 572 points and Daniel has 547. Daniel leads in goals by a wide margin, 208 to 138. Henrik has 44 playoff points, Daniel has 42. Both want to show their appreciation for the way they've been treated by Canuck fans. They want a Stanley Cup to match the gold medals they earned when Sweden won the 2006 Olympic hockey title.

The Canucks save the captaincy announcement for just before opening game. Henrik has big boots to fill because the Vancouver captaincy has been awarded previously to Orland Kurtenbach, Andre Boudrias, Chris Oddleifson, Don Lever, Kevin McCarthy, Stan Smyl,

Dan Quinn, Doug Lidster, Trevor Linden, Mark Messier, Markus Naslund and Luongo. Some have shared the captaincy with others players in the same year; Smyl was captain the longest, serving from the 1982–83 season until 1989–90. Kurtenbach, Smyl and Linden are still considered the consummate captains. Henrik Sedin, with his brother Daniel an assistant, has a new challenge: lead the team back to the playoffs and deeper into the post-season.

Manny Malhotra, signed in the off-season through free agency, quickly grows to appreciate the Sedins just like other teammates have over the years. He likes the fact that they rarely talk about themselves, preferring to change the subject when their names come up. Malhotra

Right winger Alex Burrows came back from off-season shoulder surgery to score 26 goals, solidifying his place on the top line. RIC ERNST/PNG

observes that on good teams, the internal focus is not on individuals, but rather on the system and the culture that makes team goals accessible. The Sedins were brought up in a household with two older brothers, Peter and Stefan. They were role models for Henrik and Daniel. When they were young, the twins were invited to play pickup hockey games with their brothers because the Sedin family was raised to include everyone in activities. Perhaps that explains their passion for playmaking on the ice.

And to the Vancouver community, the Sedins are a genuine gift that keeps on giving. They have shown their profound appreciation for the local area by generously donating $1.5 million to the pediatric intensive care unit and diagnostic imaging area at BC Children's Hospital. The Canucks have reaped many benefits from the abilities of the Sedins, but for some reason hockey fans in the Vancouver area always expect more, and that's okay with the twins. They are giving people and have a desire to oblige.

The Canucks begin the season on October 9 against Los Angeles, dropping a 2–1 decision in overtime when the Kings win the shootout. Two nights later, Daniel Sedin scores twice in a 2–1 decision over the Florida Panthers. Daniel scores in each of the next two games, giving him four goals in four games, and he's off to the races, trying to duplicate his brother's feat of winning the Art Ross Trophy awarded to the NHL scoring champion. The twins have a remarkable knack of being able to find each other with pinpoint passes. Sometimes it's on line rushes, or more often than not when they start a cycle in one of the corners near the opposing net. They are uncanny with their anticipation. Daniel shoots more accurately off the pass than Henrik, while Henrik is particularly adept at making backhand passes through a maze of legs. One thing is certain: they'll always insist they come to the rink every day expecting to play the same way. They don't change, but just increase their proficiency. They try to take small steps ahead each season, working out a little harder in the off-season when they elevate their skills to an even higher level.

New teammate Keith Ballard observes players fall in line with the attitude and demeanour of the Sedins. They play hard, whistle to whistle, then get to the bench without much further ado. It's the type of approach Gillis and Vigneault want from Kesler and Burrows. In other words, less trash talk after whistles. It's something Burrows and Kesler plan to be better at this season. Vigneault concedes in his personable way that the Sedins are pretty extraordinary and the Canucks are fortunate to have them in Vancouver. They are the team's role models for consistency. They are poised, quiet and clinical in approach. And, they're signed through the 2013–14 season, each with an average salary of $6.1 million per season.

As the season progresses, it becomes evident Kesler and Burrows have taken to heart the suggestion they concentrate on playing without trash talking. Burrows returns to the lineup on November 2 against the Edmonton Oilers, his shoulder intact once again. It takes the right winger five games to regain his scoring touch. He produces his first goal on November 11 against the Ottawa Senators. The Canucks win 6–2 in the nation's capital and Daniel Sedin scores also. So does rookie Mario

Bliznak, called up from the minors to bolster the line-up during a five-game road trip with stops in Montreal, Ottawa, Toronto, Buffalo and Pittsburgh.

The Canucks return home with two wins under their belt. They lose the final game of the road trip in Pittsburgh and return to Rogers Arena to face archrival Chicago. The Blackhawks aren't the same team as a year ago, most people concede, but still have many top offensive weapons. They turn them loose against Vancouver and the home team leaves the ice on November 20 with their egos bruised after a humbling 7–1 defeat. The next night, the Canucks lose again at home, this time 3–2 against the Phoenix

Spectacular collision between Canucks winger Jeff Tambellini and Mark Giordano of the Calgary Flames in regular season action at Rogers Arena. STEVE BOSCH/PNG

Coyotes. Vigneault and his coaching staff are outwardly calm, but internally they plan a regrouping, understanding their team must stop playing so loose defensively. Henrik Sedin seizes the moment to show why he was selected captain. He calls a team meeting and players air their opinions.

Vancouver's next opponent is the Colorado Avalanche, which has hired 1994 Canucks playoff star Kirk McLean as a goaltending consultant. McLean attracts some local attention working with Craig Anderson and Peter Budaj during the morning skate, but come game time, it is all Canucks as Kevin Bieksa, Daniel Sedin, Burrows and Kesler score goals to kick-start a four-game winning streak that includes a 3–0 shutout for Luongo in Chicago.

The Canucks then lose their next game at home against the St. Louis Blues, but proceed to go on an incredible string of seventeen games without losing a game in regulation time. All the pieces fall in place for Vigneault and his staff from December 8 to January 11. Vancouver finally loses on January 13 in New York against the Rangers, but the month-long winning streak establishes the Canucks as legitimate contenders for the Western Conference title.

"Everybody finds a way to contribute on this team, that's the nice thing about it," Luongo opines. "It's not always the same guy." No, it's the combination of Luongo and the rookie Schneider in goal, plus a defence that features the rushing and shooting of Christian Ehrhoff, plus the defensive pairing of Bieksa and Hamhuis that provides Vancouver with a shut-down duo to match against the top opposing players.

Vigneault is pushing all the right buttons, even when there are scoring slumps.

As the season progresses, Mason Raymond and Mikael Samuelsson experience injuries and struggle to score. No matter, as second-line centre Kesler picks up the slack. Kesler skates like the wind most nights, using a combination of speed, size and a whistling wrist shot to score more goals than ever before. Kesler has gained league-wide recognition for his two-way play. He's always been a reliable defensive player by blocking shots, winning faceoffs and picking up his man in the Vancouver zone. Now his offensive game is becoming a key factor in the success of the Canucks. Vancouver drafted the Michigan-born Kesler in the first round in 2003 following his one season at Ohio State University. He was projected as a third-line centreman, a player capable of being an irritant to the opposition.

"He skated so well," recalls Stan Smyl, who coached the developing Kesler when they were with the Manitoba Moose in the American Hockey League. "We found that Ryan was going to be a special player. Ryan has the size and skill, not just the skating ability, to do many different things. We learned quickly to put trust in him. He adjusted to the pro game after college and earned his ice time, in the minors and at the NHL level. He has such a great passion for the game and it gets him the respect he rightly deserves."

Kesler's game evolves every season. He scored twenty-five goals

Second-line centre Ryan Kesler screens Canadiens' Carey Price February 22 at Rogers Arena. Kesler had a career year, scoring 41 goals while winning the Selke Trophy for best defensive play by a forward. STEVE BOSCH/PNG

the previous season and now he's headed for his first NHL season of over forty goals. No longer is Kesler considered only a checking centre. He draws more attention from other teams because he's constantly a pain in the neck at both ends of the ice. "He's the complete package, just like Mike Richards," says Ron Delorme, chief amateur scout for the Canucks and part of the draft team that selected Kesler. "He's special. Ryan can surprise you with his creativity and, just like Stan Smyl had, he has the heart of a lion." Kesler earned a gold medal with the United States team at the World Junior Championship in 2004 and added an Olympic silver medal at the Vancouver Olympics in 2010. Now he wants the Canucks to enjoy the same type of success in their quest for the Stanley Cup.

Another positive development for the Canucks is the play of Schneider, the backup goaltender who appears to have what it takes to be a future NHL star. Schneider is providing the Canucks with quality starts during the regular season, giving Luongo the amount of time off that management desires. Schneider was selected twenty-sixth overall in the 2004 draft, a year after Kesler. He's from Marblehead, Maine, near Boston and attended Boston College for three years before turning professional with Vancouver's farm club in Manitoba. He played ten NHL games over two seasons before earning regular employment with the Canucks in the fall of 2010. "I'm feeling really comfortable at this level," Schneider confides. "I'm in a great situation, on a winning team with a great group of guys."

Schneider has learned how to be patient, to bide his time after three years in college and three more in the minors. He's appreciative of learning from Luongo and goalie coach Roland Melanson. He doesn't let the future bother him because he knows that first he must prove himself at the NHL level. As it turns out, the netminders picked ahead of Schneider in the 2004 draft haven't been quite as fortunate. Al Montoya went sixth overall and struggled in the New York Rangers organization before eventually landing nearby with the Islanders. Devan Dubnyk was selected fourteenth overall by Edmonton

Goal prospect Cory Schneider had a promising year under the tutelage of new goaltending coach Roland Melanson, amassing a 16–4 record in 25 games. RIC ERNST/PNG

and is just settling into more regular playing time, albeit playing behind a much different defence than Schneider. The seventeenth choice that year was Marek Schwartz of the junior Vancouver Giants, taken by the St. Louis Blues. He's back playing in his native Czech Republic.

Schneider had some struggles during the Vancouver pre-season, especially during an eight-goal drubbing by Edmonton. He managed to regroup and was ready for the regular season. His first start came against Carolina Hurricanes on October 17 and Schneider came away a 5–1 winner. The focus for Schneider is on improvement so he can be trusted when called upon. Vigneault and Melanson seem to feel they can make that call with enough frequency to satisfy Schneider and provide Luongo with that extra rest that should be beneficial come playoff time.

The Vancouver defence has taken some hits during the season on the injury front. The Canucks began the schedule without Sami Salo after the oft-injured veteran was hurt playing a version of floor hockey during the summer back home in Finland. Vancouver begins the season with no certainty of when Salo will return, if at all, which paves the way for Bieksa to take a more prominent role. During the summer, there was speculation he would be traded because of team salary cap problems. Plus, Bieksa was heading into the final year of his contract, with unrestricted free agency on the horizon. But during the regular season, Bieksa proves himself to be one of Vancouver's most reliable players. He settles into a defensive partnership with Hamhuis and for the most part, curtails his madcap rushes up ice that in the past had hurt the team.

All the president's men

Defensive coach Rick Bowness has worked long and hard with Bieksa over the past five years and finally there's a sense that Bieksa has grasped the situation and gets what it takes to be successful. Bowness notes there's a maturity level he hasn't seen before in Bieksa, that he's more patient with himself, and that allows Bieksa to be more responsible defensively. Bowness starts using Bieksa up to twenty-five minutes a game in close contests and the results are positive. He's reliable and steady, says Bowness. Bieksa is exactly what teams look for in a defender. He skates well, he's strong and he's willing to play a physical game. His offence suffers a little when he concentrates on defence, but Bieksa still

Kevin Bieksa, right, collides with Edmonton Oilers Ryan Jones, left, during a regular season game April 2. On the bubble for much of his Canuck career, Bieksa rounded into a defensive stalwart in 2011. RIC ERNST/PNG

joins the odd rush to show he hasn't lost any of his skill with the puck. How does Bieksa explain things? "Being healthy is the first thing," Bieksa says, "and having a full training camp and a great partner on a pretty good team with good goaltending. I'm just kind of a product of that."

The rapid rise of the Canucks in the standings brings more national attention to the team, with three Vancouver players named to play in the annual NHL All-Star Game on January 30 in Raleigh, NC, home of the Carolina Hurricanes. Henrik Sedin is selected along with his brother Daniel and power-play linemate Kesler. Not picked, however, is goaltender Luongo, perhaps because of his usual slow start to the regular season. But make no mistake, Luongo is one of the best in the league at the All-Star break, perhaps overlooked because the league wants to include as many players as possible from other teams. The All-Star goalies are Tim Thomas of Boston, Marc-Andre Fleury of Pittsburgh, Jonas Hiller of Anaheim, Cam Ward of Carolina, Henrik Lundqvist of the New York Rangers and Carey Price of Montreal. All are deserving of being among the elite of the game, while for Luongo it's another opportunity to rest his bones for the final ten weeks of the regular season.

This All-Star affair features a player draft for the first time, conducted by team captains Nicklas Lidstrom from Detroit and Eric Staal of Carolina. Lidstrom takes Henrik Sedin and his team eventually wins 11–10 in the high-scoring affair where offence takes priority over defence. Daniel Sedin and Kesler play for the Staal team. The winning goaltender, for an unprecedented third straight year, is Thomas, who has regained the No. 1 job with the Bruins from Tuukka Rask.

The Sedins and Kesler return from the All-Star Game no worse for wear and the Canucks are again off to the races. They win 4–1 in Dallas when Schneider plays against the Stars to prolong Luongo's inactivity. Vancouver has Dallas's number this season as the Canucks keep coming up with timely goals, even when the opposition has more of the play. The Canuck power play has improved immensely. The Sedins are as creative as ever, but there's more variety to the attack with the man advantage. Christian Ehrhoff is dangerous with point shots and Kesler is a threat from in close. He's doing everything right all over the ice, enough for another nomination for the Frank J. Selke Trophy awarded to the forward who best excels in the defensive aspects of the game. Kesler was a finalist the previous two seasons. The award has gone to Detroit's Pavel Datsyuk for three straight years. Kesler is getting more attention than ever this season because he's scoring more goals, many of the spectacular fashion, while still being top-notch defensively.

Daniel Sedin seems headed in the same direction as brother Henrik a year ago, to the top of the NHL scoring parade where the Art Ross Trophy sits. Henrik won it in 2009–10 and now Daniel has a chance to make it a brother act. No brothers have every won the Art Ross in consecutive years. In fact, the only brothers to ever claim the Ross were Doug Bentley and Max Bentley, both with Chicago. Left winger Doug won in 1942–43 and centreman Max claimed two scoring titles, in 1945–46 and 1946–47. Naturally the Sedins say very little about the scoring race because they'd rather concentrate on another title. The Presidents' Trophy goes to the NHL team with the most points in either conference and the Canucks have never claimed the prize. With it comes home ice advantage throughout the playoffs, so it's no wonder the Sedins have their sights set on the bigger prize.

There are still some bumps in the road to be encountered. The Canucks worry about the lack of scoring from Raymond and Samuelsson. They bring up prize rookie Cody Hodgson from the minors, but he's not the answer, at least not yet. Hodgson is tentative and plays not to make mistakes, rather than asserting his offensive capabilities as a skilled forward. Vigneault rarely gives him a chance in offensive situations, though the coach does try Hodgson on the second power-play unit occasionally.

The injury bug continues to haunt the defence in the second half of the schedule. Dan Hamhuis suffers a second concussion when drilled into the glass by Anaheim captain Ryan Getzlaf. There's even a tougher time ahead when Alexander Edler learns he must undergo back surgery, plus there are injuries to Andrew Alberts and rookie Lee Sweatt. The Canucks don't like the Getzlaf hit on Hamhuis during a game in which Vancouver lost in regulation time for the first time in nearly two months. It seems just as the Canucks get one defenceman back in the lineup, another goes down.

The revolving door in front of Luongo and Schneider puts a lot of pressure on Bieksa and Ehrhoff to play more minutes. By the end of the season the Canucks will use no less than thirteen defencemen, severely testing the depth of the organization. Having a veteran like newcomer Keith Ballard certainly helps during defensive shortages, but there are growing concerns over the reliability of Ballard, who tends to be out of position when he tries to do too much. Ballard often presses to the point where his efforts are counterproductive, which hurts his credibility with the coaching staff. However, youngsters like Chris Tanev and Yann Sauve experience playing time in the NHL that enhances their development, especially Tanev.

Bowness does a masterful job holding things together with his back-end boys. They keep the goals-against respectable while Tanev develops in just his first year of pro hockey, and Sami Salo prepares for his return to duty. Salo is thirty-six and he doesn't play a game until February 12 against Calgary. Remarkably, he plays sixteen minutes and thirty-four seconds in his season debut and the Canucks beat the Flames 4–2. Salo has experienced forty-plus injuries during his NHL career, but keeps on ticking. He still has the will to play and be proficient. He's a welcome addition to the depleted defensive corps that needs a boost. There are a lot of admiring teammates after Salo overcomes an Achilles tendon tear that occurred during the summer in Finland.

It takes a lot of mental toughness to return from such a serious injury. Salo came back to Vancouver in the fall and spent endless hours working out in the weight room, mostly alone. There were so many baby steps in his rehabilitation that many wondered if he could endure such a lengthy process. The support of family, friends and teammates helped Salo through those moments when self-doubt crept in. He'd lie in bed and wonder about his future, about whether or not he'd skate again. Finally, it was time to get back on the ice. He took it

Veteran defense Sami Salo patrols the ice in front of Cory Schneider during action against the Colorado Avalanche in March. The hulking Finn reclaimed top-four pairing after surviving an epic Achilles tendon rehab. IAN LINDSAY/PNG

slowly, hoping that his Achilles tendon would heal properly. Salo wasn't ready for retirement. Part of his comeback included a brief stint in the minors with the Manitoba Moose, where he scored two goals in his very first game. Then it was back to Vancouver to wear his familiar No. 6 sweater once again. "It's been a real long road to recovery-land here, mentally and physically," Vigneault observes. "It must have been real challenging for him, but you can see in his face, he's happy to be back. He wants this opportunity."

The road back wouldn't be near as long for Edler,

who is twelve years younger than Salo. The Swedish-born Edler's constantly sore back requires microdiscec-tomy surgery to correct the back spasms that restricted his play for far too long. Edler leaves the lineup follow-ing the January 24 game against Dallas and is expected to be out for almost three months. He hopes to return during the playoffs. Instead he's back in early April for the final two games of the regular season. The silver lining to the Edler injury is that his absence gave the Canucks some much-needed salary cap room as Edler was placed on injured reserve. It allowed for the return of Salo and also the addition of two players at the NHL trading deadline.

GM Mike Gillis strikes at the last moment before the late February deadline. The Canucks acquire left wing-er Chris Higgins from the Florida Panthers and centre Maxim Lapierre from the Anaheim Ducks. Both are con-sidered depth additions that have had valuable playoff experience with the Montreal Canadiens. The Canucks did not disturb their NHL roster in adding experienced playoff skaters. It's anticipated both newcomers will start on the fourth line and, if they fit into the Vancouver system, will be able to move ahead in the pecking order when needed. Higgins has a decent touch around the net and had three straight seasons with twenty or more goals when he was with the Canadiens. Lapierre is more of a checker and agitator who is asked to curtail his trash talking, just as Burrows and Kesler were earlier in the season.

Vigneault foresees no problems in working with either player. He coached Lapierre extensively in junior. Higgins, on the other hand, came to his fourth NHL team with the trade and approaches unrestricted free agency, so he needs to put up some numbers offensively. Gillis believes it's a win-win situation for the Canucks. "If you think you're close [to a championship], you have to support it the best you can," says Gillis. "These trades make us a little bit better." One of the things that made both Higgins and Lapierre attractive to the Canucks is that both can kill penalties. Plus, Lapierre is decent on face-offs. The Canucks are one of the best, if not the best, team in the league on the draw and having another capable centreman is a luxury not all teams enjoy.

The Canucks have improved when shorthanded through the combination of speed and partnerships. The penalty-kill units work best when the same players are in

GM Gillis picked up depth forwards Maxim Lapierre and Chris Higgins right at the trade deadline. Both contributed down the stretch. RIC ERNST/PNG

partnership, especially the forwards. The Kesler-Burrows duo has been together for some time and Vancouver has another strong duo in newcomer Manny Malhotra and the fast-improving Jannik Hansen. Making the Canucks even stronger on the penalty kill is the availability of Raymond, Tanner Glass, Higgins and Lapierre, not to mention the Sedins, who can be used late in shorthanded situations and be on the ice when the Canucks return to full strength. Vancouver was ranked eighteenth in the NHL the previous season when shorthanded, so the improvement speaks volumes about why Vancouver is a serious contender for the Western Conference title.

Canuck defencemen have a lot to do with the upswing as well, as they block shots and take away passing lanes with their positioning and quick sticks. There's no Willie Mitchell to block shots this season, but there also isn't a noticeable drop-off in this regard. Kesler is always a threat to score shorthanded as the Canucks rarely hesitate to push the puck ahead and out of the defensive zone. When the faceoff men do their job and the Canucks block the shooting lanes, they get the job done shorthanded, leaving far less critical work for the goaltenders.

But late in the regular season, the Canucks take a huge hit on special teams when Malhotra, the popular centreman who fit in seamlessly, was seriously injured on March 16. A puck caroms off Malhotra's stick in neutral ice while he is being checked by Colorado's Erik Johnson and strikes the Vancouver player near his left eye. A hush comes over Rogers Arena as the bloodied Malhotra immediately leaves the ice with a towel held to the side of his face. The Canucks lose one of their most underrated players for an indefinite time. Vancouver players are unsure when Malhotra will return, if ever. Eye injuries are feared by everyone and the Canucks try not to think about the leadership that will be missed. He has surgery the next day because fluid needs to be drained from his damaged eye. The state of his vision is unknown.

"Our hope is that Manny will come out of this and be absolutely 100 percent and be able to continue on where he left off," GM Gillis carefully states. "We're

One of the low points in an otherwise great season came when durable forward Manny Malhotra was hustled off the ice holding a towel to his head. It was a dreaded eye injury, and it deprived Vancouver of a key player heading into the playoffs.

MARK VAN MANEN/PNG

waiting for more information. We simply don't know." The Canucks have experienced a major eye injury before when defenceman Mattias Ohlund was struck by a shot in a 1999 pre-season game in Ottawa. Ohlund missed parts of two seasons following surgery and never regained full peripheral vision in his right eye. The popular Ohlund continued his career with Vancouver until signing with the Tampa Bay Lightning as a free agent in 2009.

Teammates describe Malhotra as a "first-class individual" who brings a distinct level of professionalism to the team. In the summer, after signing as a free agent, he helped organize informal team skates for conditioning purposes. Raffi Torres played alongside the Toronto-born Malhotra when they were with the Columbus Blue Jackets and has a deep respect for Malhotra's commitment and outlook. "He always has these words of wisdom and every time you see him, you just want to start asking him things," says Torres. "You just want to know what he's thinking because you know he's a step above."

The entire Canucks family is thinking about Malhotra when he leaves for New York and more surgery. The news is better, but a return is far from certain. So the cruise through the regular season gets a little rougher without Malhotra. Raymond is auditioned as a third-line centreman, but it's hardly a success. Raymond can skate and handle the puck, but his playmaking, especially when he's on his backhand, leaves plenty to be desired. The newcomer Lapierre is a possibility, but first it seems Vigneault must exhaust other possibilities.

The Canucks continue on their merry way toward first place in the NHL West. They clinch the Northwest

Division title the same night as the Malhotra injury when they beat the Avalanche 4–2 on two goals by Henrik Sedin and one each by Lapierre and Burrows. Vancouver earns the Western Conference crown on March 29 with a 3–1 win in Nashville on two goals by Burrows and another from Aaron Rome into an empty net. There's just one little matter still to be addressed.

In their next game two nights later in Vancouver, the Canucks claim their first Presidents' Trophy as the overall NHL regular-season points leader by beating the Los Angeles Kings 3–1 on goals by season-long stalwarts Daniel Sedin, Ehrhoff and Kesler. But for Sedin, the job is only just beginning. "Ninety-five percent of this team has been through playoff failure and we don't want to be part of that anymore," says Daniel. "We're focused every game on playing the right way and that can't change in the playoffs. We don't need to do anything extra—just go out there and take care of business."

Injured Canuck Manny Malhotra helps captain Henrik Sedin 33 accept the second best prize in hockey—the Presidents' Trophy for the best team in the regular season, Rogers Arena, April 7, 2011. MARK VAN MANEN/PNG

## CHAPTER THREE

*"We kept pushing and knew it was going to
come. We knew it was our time."*
—Ryan Kesler sums up a showdown
with the Blackhawks

Slaying the dragon

Vancouver's first-round playoff opponent turns out to
be Chicago after the Blackhawks slip into eighth place
courtesy of a Dallas loss in the last game of the regular
season. Chicago was also beaten that day by Detroit, so
all the Stars had to do was win a later game on the road
against Minnesota. The Wild would finish out of the
playoffs, but on that day had other ideas as Minnesota
won easily, forcing Dallas coach Marc Crawford to the
outside looking in at the playoffs. Chicago qualified
through the back door for an opportunity to defend the
Stanley Cup championship.

The Canucks might have wanted another opponent—they dominated Dallas all season long, never losing
a game to the Stars—but settled for a chance at redemp-
tion against a team that had eliminated Vancouver the
past two post-seasons. The matchup went to six games
both two years, and the teams split their four games

the past regular season, so everything points to a long series. "We know it's not going to be an easy task," offers Canucks netminder Roberto Luongo, who has had his struggles against the Blackhawks. "We're playing the champions and that's the first thing that comes to mind. But we have another year under our belts as far as experience and maturity, and we feel we're ready to take that next step."

Only this time the Canucks seem to have a few more bullets than the Blackhawks. Daniel Sedin is the NHL scoring champion after a 104-point season, including 41 goals. Team captain Henrik Sedin leads the league in assists with 75. Ryan Kesler is a 41-goal scorer, giving Vancouver two 40-plus snipers, while Chicago has none. The Blackhawks are led by captain Jonathan Toews and his 76 points. Patrick Sharp is the top goal scorer with 34 after missing eight games late in the season with a knee injury. Talented winger Patrick Kane produced 73 points.

In goal, the Canucks should have the edge because Luongo and netminding partner Cory Schneider have earned the William M. Jennings Trophy by allowing the fewest goals as a team during the regular season. Chicago has rookie Corey Crawford in goal after he claimed the No. 1 spot from fading veteran Marty Turco. Both teams have defencemen that can produce points. Brent Seabrook had forty-eight for Chicago and Duncan Keith another forty-five. The Canucks blue-line brigade is led by Christian Ehrhoff with fifty. Keith and Seabrook are durable, both having played all eighty-two regular season games. The Canucks do not have a defenceman who played every game before the playoffs.

"We're not worried a whole lot about the last couple of years," ventures Canuck defender Kevin Bieksa before Game 1. "Obviously we have a history with Chicago, but it's a different team for them. They lost a lot of key guys, but more importantly, we have a whole new mentality. I could care less about what guys they are missing. It will be intense, no matter who they lace up." Yes, the Blackhawks are much different. Salary cap problems forced Chicago general manager Stan Bowman to unload almost half his team, including much of the team's true grit. Gone from the year before are Dustin Byfuglien, Kris Versteeg, Andrew Ladd, Brent Sopel, John Madden, Adam Burish, Ben Eager, Nick Boynton, Colin Fraser and Jordan Hendry, plus goaltenders Antti Niemi and Cristobal Huet. The replacements are decent, but cheaper also means not as good.

Defenceman Christian Ehrhoff in a rare scrap with Victor Stalberg of Chicago. Ehrhoff was too busy racking up a career-high 50 points to do much of this. IAN LINDSAY/PNG

The Canucks have changed also, but not nearly to the extent of Chicago. Plus, the Blackhawks go into the playoffs with Troy Brouwer and David Bolland on the limp. Vancouver seems to have an advantage with the return of Sami Salo and Alexander Edler on defence, the addition of Dan Hamhuis and the presence of Luongo in goal. Vancouver also has a definite statistical edge as the Canucks were first in the NHL in goals scored with a 3.15 average, lowest goals-against at 2.20, first on the power play with 24.3 percent efficiency, tied for second on the penalty-kill at 85.6 percent, and first in faceoffs, winning 54.9 percent of draws.

Before the series, Kesler and Burrows talk about how they've both changed, how they are better equipped to handle the trash talking of players like Bolland. There seems to be more of an even keel to the Vancouver team than a year ago, a refreshing approach that means business before B.S. Last year Burrows and Kesler were forced to play through shoulder injuries. Now they're healthy, happy and raring to go, to prove Vancouver deserves the No. 1 ranking that goes with the Presidents' Trophy.

Two of Vancouver's forward prospects will get their NHL playoff baptism against the Blackhawks. Cody Hodgson, a centre, and right winger Victor Oreskovich are summoned from the Manitoba Moose. The Canucks want them involved in the post-season, even if it's only for a few shifts a game. With Raffi Torres sitting out the first two playoff games to complete his four-game suspension for a high hit on Edmonton's Jordan Eberle in the eightieth game of the regular season, the Canucks have an opportunity to test their organizational depth. Even with all the late-season injuries the Canucks had, they still managed to maintain their consistency over the long haul.

Canucks winger Mikael Samuelsson has been to the Stanley Cup final before and earned a championship ring with the Detroit Red Wings. He cautions Vancouver teammates about feeling too good about themselves before the playoffs. "We still have to prove it on the ice," Samuelsson says. "It's a thin, thin line. Things can happen. You have to have emotions, but in the right way. You can't take any stupid penalties." In other words, respect you opponent. There may not be a Byfuglien to crash the crease and disrupt Luongo, but someone else could emerge in that role, perhaps someone like Tomas Kopecky.

Canucks coach Alain Vigneault preaches that his team has learned its lessons well enough to be considered a legitimate title contender. "I think if you learn from the past there's a good chance the future will be different," Vigneault says before the first playoff game. "We think we have proven a lot of things during the regular season. Now it's our turn to go try and prove it in the playoffs." Bieksa lets it be known that he respects Chicago, but at the same time admits a hatred of the opposition is evident when the jersey goes on and the game begins. "It's a team we want to beat badly," he says. The Vancouver coaches want Bieksa and Dan Hamhuis on defence, with Kesler at centre, when the Blackhawks have Toews on the ice. It's the best possible matchup for the Canucks.

Game 1 of the 2011 playoffs, on April 13, sees Chicago coach Joel Quenneville start with Toews at centre between wingers Marian Hossa and Patrick Sharp.

The Canucks go with a forward line of Kesler, Chris Higgins and Samuelsson, with Hamhuis and Bieksa on defence. The matching game is underway. On the second shift Vigneault uses Henrik and Daniel Sedin with Alex Burrows. Chicago counters with Seabrook and Keith on defence and a forward line of Michael Frolik, Kane and rookie Ben Smith. Both coaches get the matchups they want without too much disruption.

Vancouver sets the early tempo and has a strong first period. Higgins scores the first goal of the series when he tips in a point shot by Bieksa at 7:03, beating Crawford high on the stick side. Crawford faces thirteen shots in the first period and seems jittery. He fails to leave his net for a loose puck inside the Chicago blue line and is beaten on a breakaway by Jannik Hansen. Should Crawford have come out for the puck? Probably. At the other end Luongo looks supremely confident. He kicks out his right leg for a brilliant pad save against rushing Blackhawks defenceman Brian Campbell. Vancouver leads 2–0 after one period. The Canucks dress Hodgson and Oreskovich and they play limited roles. Hodgson starts on the third line with Mason Raymond and Hansen, but is used sparingly. As the game progresses, Maxim Lapierre gets more and more time on the third line. It is clear Vigneault doesn't want to overexpose the rookies.

In the second period the Canucks play more defensively, hanging back to make sure Chicago doesn't get a numbers advantage on rushes. Chicago plays a little better and gets a lift from Kane, who shifts from line to line, depending on the situation. Kane slams his stick on the ice in disgust at one stage after Luongo makes a

spectacular save on Sharp by batting the puck out of the air with his goal stick.

Vancouver becomes more determined in the third period, with defenceman Alexander Edler playing an extremely physical game. He finishes with seven hits, one less than Lapierre, who clearly wants third-line ice time. Chicago loses winger Kopecky with an injury and later Blackhawks centre Ryan Johnson is shaken on a hard hit delivered by Glass. The Canucks are confident and sure of themselves in the opener. The Rogers Arena crowd jeers Crawford by serenading "We want Turco," as the backup netminder sits at the end of the bench. Chicago is not nearly as physical as the last two years and Vancouver wins 2–0. "I don't know if it's a statement, but we had a lot of emotion in the building and we're trying to feed off that," summarizes Hansen. "We wanted to get off to a good start. That was a way to do it."

The Canucks draw first blood without the Sedins getting a single point. Luongo used his size-fifteen skate to make a huge save on Campbell. "Our line didn't play our best game," admits Henrik Sedin. "But we have a lot of other guys who can score goals. That is going to be a key for us." Vigneault acknowledges the Canucks wanted to establish their physical game, especially putting pressure on Keith in trying to eliminate some of his rushes up ice. Without Keith and Campbell jumping into the attack, it's much more difficult for the Blackhawks to create odd-man rushes.

Jannik Hansen celebrates his breakaway goal against Corey Crawford in Game 1 of the Chicago series. RIC ERNST/PNG

55

Hodgson may have struggled, but Oreskovich left his mark with a couple bone-crushing hits. Oreskovich had fourteen shifts and four hits during his nine minutes and forty-eight seconds. Hodgson was given twelve shifts for 7:38 and was credited with one hit. Vigneault elected to dress Keith Ballard on defence and sit out Aaron Rome. The sometimes error-prone Ballard didn't hurt the Canucks as he plays a safe game with partner Sami Salo. Lapierre was Vancouver's leading hitter in Game 1 and was pleased with his role, which has grown since the Malhotra injury. He's keeping his mouth shut and just playing the game, finishing his checks with his stick on the ice, as the coaches have asked. "Play between the whistles," is his mindset after eight hits in eighteen shifts.

Before the second game, Quenneville admits the Blackhawks must have more of a net presence in front of Luongo, believing the Canucks netminder had a clear view of most of the shots in the opener. The Chicago coach wants Luongo to have to work harder, to have a more difficult time seeing point shots launched by great shooters like Keith, Seabrook and Campbell. Quenneville is fully aware of what made his team successful against Vancouver the previous two years. The difference now is that he has to convince several of the newer players that they must do the gritty things in order to be successful. "They deserved to win Game 1," Quenneville says. "Now we've got to counter-punch them. Playoffs, you've got to adapt to each game, change the way you play. We know how to fix our game."

One down, three to go. Canucks surround Luongo and fans wave white towels as the Blackhawks fall 2–0 in Game 1.

RIC ERNST/PNG

In the Canuck dressing room, the Canucks aren't buying into the suggestion Chicago was tired in the opener after playing several stressful games in eight days in order to get into the playoffs. Vancouver has learned in recent years just how resilient the Blackhawks can be. The Canucks are pleased with the play of Edler in just his third game back in the lineup following surgery. Edler has manned up, using his 6-foot-4 frame to hand out jolting bodychecks in the opener to Frolik and Bryan Bickell, separating them from the puck. The Vancouver coaching staff notes that there was no hesitation on Edler's part to avoid contact. Edler says his back feels stronger than ever and his conditioning is improving. "A lot of people see a big, Swedish defenceman and they think they're not going to get hit," Ballard offers about Edler. "But he's so big and so physical, and you watch him skate and it's effortless. He is the total package."

Game 2 in Vancouver starts a lot like the opener, with the Canucks scoring the first goal, again from an unlikely source. This time it's Hansen pulling the trigger with a little help from both Sedins. The twenty-five-year-old Dane converts a setup from Daniel with the greatest of ease as the depth of the Canucks keeps the Blackhawks at bay. "There's not a lot of room for error," Hansen says later, noting that checkers like himself can't afford to miss on their few scoring chances. "Our main concern is to keep the other guys from scoring. If we do manage to chip one in, it's a big advantage."

The second period also belongs to the Canucks as Daniel Sedin scores on a power play and, after a Chicago goal by the rookie Smith, Vancouver again takes a two-goal lead on a marker from defenceman Edler, with the rookie Hodgson assisting. Again, depth is paying huge dividends. However, it's not clear sailing for Vancouver in the third period as the Blackhawks are determined to make a series of it. Viktor Stalberg, acquired from Toronto in the Versteeg trade, scores early in the third before the Canucks again have a two-goal lead on the second of the game from Daniel Sedin. Chicago makes it close on another goal by Smith before Luongo closes the door. The Canucks win 4–3 for a two-game lead as the series moves back to Chicago. The Blackhawks have yet to establish their physical presence after only four penalties were called in Game 2, two to each team. Vancouver scored on the power play and Chicago didn't.

Vancouver played without Samuelsson, who is believed to be ill, though he's had problems with nagging injuries all season. Vigneault elects to use defenceman Aaron Rome as the twelfth forward and

Even buses got into the act. WARD PERRIN/PNG

the popular Rome proves useful in a substitute role playing an unfamiliar position. The Canucks have not trailed in the series, but still haven't played their best hockey, though they deserve credit for keeping Toews off the score sheet for 120 minutes, which handicaps the Chicago offence to no end. Toews did not have a shot on goal during his twenty-two-plus minutes of ice time in Game 2. "We are doing a good job on their big guys right now," Bieksa says. "We are hoping to frustrate them and are playing those guys hard. It's not just one or two guys on our team. It's everybody finishing those guys and making it difficult." Hansen likes the fact he's getting extra shifts with the more skilled players as Vigneault rewards his lesser lights for their diligence. Hansen is considered a prolific scorer in practice by teammates, who quickly praise him for his finishing touch against Chicago.

The Canucks head to Chicago knowing their lineup will be fortified by the addition of Raffi Torres, who has sat out his four-game suspension as mandated by the league. Vigneault has a hunch that Torres won't back off his physical play. "He's a physical, energy guy and that part of his game is not going to change," predicts Vigneault. "We all know Raffi. He won't be gun-shy." Naturally, Torres agrees. "The main thing is not to lose my head out there. If the hit's there, I'll throw the hit. I want to be sound positionally and play smart." Torres has playoff experience, including a trip to the Stanley Cup final in 2006 with the Edmonton Oilers. He played twenty-two post-season games that year and produced four goals and eleven points to go with sixteen minutes in penalties. A year ago, he dressed for the Buffalo

Sabres and appeared in four playoff games. "At the end of the day I'm going to be throwing the body out there," Torres adds before his first playoff game of 2011. "I'm sure [referees] know they've got to keep an extra eye on me, but if I just go out and play hockey, I should be okay."

Samuelsson and Torres both return to the Vancouver lineup for the third game against Chicago, with Rome and Hodgson assigned to the press box. The Canucks have arguably their strongest lineup in some time. Chicago counters by dressing 6-foot-8 defenceman John Scott, an enforcer of some repute. Quenneville wants more of a physical presence in front of netminder Crawford at the United Center. The Blackhawks finally get a lead in the series when defenceman Keith scores in the first period following a faceoff win by Toews. Chicago fans get a chance to hear their theme song, "Chelsea Dagger" by the Fratellis, a tune the Canucks already despise.

The Canucks battle back in the second period when Ehrhoff scores on a power play after Henrik Sedin wins a faceoff, collects the puck along the boards and makes the pass to the point. Then it is Daniel Sedin's turn. The Canucks score in transition when Sedin is in perfect position at the far post to accept a pass from Edler for a 2–1 lead. Chicago doesn't fold its tent as the Blackhawks score on the power play for the first time in the series, with Sharp getting the tying goal after the rambunctious Torres is penalized for the second time in less than two periods.

Vigneault keeps using Torres in the third period and Torres isn't finished with his aggressive deeds. He angers the Blackhawks and the howling Chicago crowd with a thunderous hit on Seabrook behind the Hawks' net. There is no penalty call from referees Brad Watson and Greg Kimmerly as the hit goes unpunished. Quenneville and the Blackhawks are irate as Seabrook is assisted off the ice, woozy and unstable. He had his head down when hit by Torres. Was there any intent to injure? Only Torres can answer that burning question.

Meanwhile, the Canucks resume their quest for a three-game lead in the series and get their wish when Samuelsson scores on a rebound at 6:48 of the third after Crawford stops Henrik Sedin and Ehrhoff. Luongo blocks all seven shots he faces in the final period and the Canucks win 3–2 for a stranglehold in the series. They seem to be in command and poised for a series sweep after Luongo stops six shots by Kane to frustrate the young Chicago winger.

After the game, Chicago captain Toews unexpectedly decides to vent his frustrations when he speaks up about the opposition. "Everyone wants to look at the stats all year and talk about what they do well and how good a team they are," Toews says in the Chicago locker room. "That's what's frustrating. We're not exposing them for what they really are. I think a lot of people outside this locker room are giving them too much credit. Maybe we are as well. We know that we can be a better team and we just haven't shown it yet."

Luongo has played his best game of the series, considering the Canucks were shorthanded seven times. He's made his best saves against Chicago's top players, namely Kane, Sharp and Toews, players who almost owned Luongo in the spring playoffs of 2009 and 2010. "Staying deep in the net, it gives me a chance, what can

I say?" Luongo intones about his revised goalkeeping style.

Much of the post-game rhetoric revolves around Torres and the huge hit on Seabrook. Many in the Chicago media call for a lengthy suspension. The Canucks don't agree. Seabrook, who returned to play two more shifts after the incident and was hit twice before retiring for further assessment, acknowledges that

Vancouver Canucks' Sami Salo, left, battles with Chicago Blackhawks Patrick Sharp, centre, in front of goalie Roberto Luongo, right, during the first period of Game 2 against Chicago. STUART DAVIS/PNG

Torres is a hard-nosed player. "I didn't think it was a penalty," says Vigneault after looking at video. "It's a collision sport with a lot of intensity and you're walking a fine line." Vancouver defenceman Keith Ballard was on the ice for the Torres crunch and opines that Torres hit Seabrook with a shoulder when the puck was near the feet of the Chicago defenceman. "I know they're trying to take away some of these hits [to the head] and I'm for taking the dirty hits out of the game," says Ballard. "But there's a responsibility to have your head up and take the hit as well."

Daniel Sedin is confused by the whole situation: "What's wrong, what's right? Seabrook has his head down. I don't think Raffi does anything wrong. We don't know, you don't know and I don't know if the referees know." Torres now must wait for the league to decide if there's another suspension from NHL head disciplinarian Colin Campbell. He hopes not because the Canucks are playing a physical game, his kind of hockey after he plays nine minutes and seven seconds. Also in Game 3, Ballard and Hamhuis both throw huge checks, especially Hamhuis when he cartwheels Chicago rookie Marcus Kruger with a hip check. "It makes them think twice about carrying the puck when we've got guys stepping up and making hits," Hamhuis notes.

Chicago forward Sharp says there shouldn't be complaining about hitting as long as it's clean. He respects hitters and mentions Hamhuis and Edler, along with Chicago teammates Seabrook and Brouwer. "There have been a number of big hits in this series," Sharp says in reference to Hamhuis, Edler, Seabrook and Brouwer. "Those are all clean hits, part of playoff hockey. That is fun. That is what the game is about. I just think if you are going out there and trying to hurt people, that's not the way to play."

The NHL elects not to suspend Torres, giving him a mulligan after he sat out four games for the high hit on Edmonton's Eberle. This time Campbell rules that Torres has checked Seabrook in the so-called "hitting area" behind the net. NHL Rule 48 regarding head shots will not be applied. "The league had a good look at the hit and saw what a lot of guys on the ice saw," says Canuck captain Henrik Sedin. "It's one of those things where you have to be accountable [and] know where guys are on the ice." Quenneville had wanted a major penalty assessed to Torres in Game 3, but later accepted the NHL's ruling as he prepared his team for Game 4. Quenneville carefully picks his words when noting, "You definitely use it as motivation when your teammate is taking a cheap shot like that."

As the saying goes, the Blackhawks have their backs to the wall. The defending Stanley Cup champions are on the verge of being swept from the playoffs. They've been out-hit, out-scored and mostly out-played. The Canucks and Torres have drawn a line in the sand. How will the Blackhawks respond? Quenneville decides it's time for super-pest Dave Bolland to return to the lineup after being out for seventeen games with a concussion. He terrorized the Canucks last year, especially the Sedins, with his chippy, cheeky play.

Game 4 begins with two early goals. Bickell scores for Chicago when he stickhandles around Luongo for an easy tally. The Canucks answer on the power play when Salo blasts home a shot from the point. The Blackhawks are playing balls-out hockey and now they have a take-no-prisoners attitude. Keith is all over the ice and takes penalties against Hansen and Torres. The Canucks are outshot 13–7 in the first period and are on their heels. The effort isn't there, as if they're hoping Chicago will roll over and head for the golf course.

The Blackhawks come out with fire in their eyes in the second period and score four unanswered goals. Vigneault and the Canucks have no answer for this onslaught. The Sedins are on the ice for three goals against. Campbell joins the rush to score the go-ahead goal for Chicago, with no Vancouver forward back to pick up the extra attacker. Vancouver defenceman Edler falls on the next goal, allowing Keith to score on an open shot from the slot area. Bolland makes sure the Canucks know he's in the game, scoring when he skates around Luongo following a turnover by Glass. Frolik completes the second-period outburst with a breakaway goal following a bad decision by Hamhuis in neutral ice.

The wheels have fallen off the Vancouver bandwagon. Vigneault strangely elects to keep Luongo in goal to start the third, maybe praying a comeback is possible. It doesn't happen. Sharp makes it 6–1 early in the third period on a power play when he's the uncovered trailer on a rush and converts a pass from Kane. Luongo gets the hook at 2:49 of the third and Cory Schneider gets his introduction to NHL playoff hockey. He stops six of seven shots, beaten only by Sharp when the Chicago player is left unchecked at the side of the net.

After several misconduct penalties to both teams later in the third, the Canucks further illustrate their frustration when Bieksa gets into a fight and lays a beating on Stalberg. Bieksa is upset because he thinks Stalberg speared Lapierre with no penalty called. Vancouver scores a meaningless goal late in the game when Daniel Sedin gets a power-play marker against Crawford, but with a final score of 7–2 Crawford is definitely superior to Luongo.

Vancouver was unprepared to sweep the series. There were gaping holes in their defensive coverage in neutral ice, allowing Chicago easy entry into the Canuck zone. Bolland gets four points in his return, assuring he'll play at least one more game this season when the series returns to Vancouver for Game 5. The Canucks suddenly are in regroup mode, even though they lead the best-of-seven set 3–1. They should be worried because Chicago suddenly has a higher competition level. "They were hungrier than we were and you saw the result," Glass says. "They out-competed us in almost all aspects." Vigneault tries to put a positive spin on things during his post-game press conference in Chicago when he says, "It's all about work ethic. We can fix that easily."

The Vancouver defence took a beating in Game 4, partly because there wasn't enough support from the forwards. Instead of breaking up plays at the blue line as they had earlier in the series, the Canucks were backing off and giving Chicago puck carriers far too much time and space. Luongo lets in six goals on twenty-eight shots, but insists he's not going to beat himself up mentally over his performance, which resembled several he experienced the previous two years against Chicago. "There wasn't a lack of confidence," Luongo says about himself. "I'm going to put it behind me and move on. The good news is I don't have to sit on it for five months before we get to play again. We're a team that has overcome a lot of things." Bieksa tries to sum up the feelings of most teammates when he says the Canucks struggled, not Luongo. "We'll regroup and learn from our mistakes," Bieksa says. "There are plenty of them."

One thing is certain: Torres acted as a lightning rod for the Blackhawks when he ran roughshod over

Alex Edler takes the body to Chicago's Michael Frolik in Game 2 of the quarter final at Rogers Arena. RIC ERNST/PNG

Seabrook in Game 3. Seabrook did not dress for the fourth game, while Torres played ineffectively, with one hit all game. He had a brief stare-down with the behemoth Scott and both were tossed from the game with misconducts. "There was a lot of motivation for our team," Toews says about facing elimination. "We wanted to play for each other. We wanted to play for guys like Seabs, considering what happened the game before. In a way, it was kind of our way of showing a little payback. It kind of added insult to injury when we don't get the decision we want [from the League]. We didn't feel [Torres] should be in the game tonight."

Meanwhile, the Chicago crowd got into the act during Game 4 when verbal abuse was directed at Vancouver GM Gillis and other Canuck executives as they were seated near excitable fans at the United Center. The foul language resulted in exchanges that didn't die down until the game was over. Torres broke his silence between games when the red-headed winger spoke for the first time since the Seabrook incident, noting that sometimes it's a good thing to take your lumps and go through a one-sided defeat. "Before you can become a champion, you have to learn how to lose," Torres says. "It was a tough loss, but it's behind us. We've learned from it." Have they really?

When the Canucks return home, defenceman Salo plays the role of elder statesman, which he is at age thirty-six. He reminds everyone that the Canucks need to return to playing their style and not to worry so much about what the critics say following one loss in Chicago. The focus can only be only the next game, Salo says, not on what happened the previous game. "We just weren't ready last game, it's as easy as that," states Salo. "Time to move on."

The Canucks to a man seem sure that Luongo will regain his form after a dismal outing. Collectively they realize the entire team has to pick up the pace after a 7–2 drubbing. Vigneault allows Luongo, Henrik Sedin and Edler to miss practice, insisting it's merely extra rest time. Not everyone buys it and some insiders wonder if there are unreported injuries at play. Vigneault does admit the Canucks have to be better at line changes as his players were caught being slow off the bench several times in Chicago. Another topic of between-games discussion is Bolland, who clearly enjoys making life miserable for the Sedins. Daniel admits Bolland is a good player and perhaps underrated when he says the Canucks must play against Bolland like they do against Toews, Kane and Sharp.

Chicago now has three proficient centremen to call upon in Toews, Sharp and Bolland. Quenneville can be a little more creative with his matchups, leaving Bolland to do the dirty work against the Sedins. Still, the Canucks have home ice advantage in Game 5 and believe it will make a difference. Vancouver players are in agreement they need to have more of a physical presence again, just like they did earlier in the series. "In the first few games we did a good job crowding them and frustrating them," Bieksa says. "When they start making plays, it backs us off a little bit."

The Blackhawks make sure they keep it up in Game 5 at Vancouver when they completely dominate the Canucks by an embarrassing 5–0 differential. Crawford gets the shutout and Luongo is pulled again, this time early in the second period after being beaten four times. The Canucks play Rome on defence in Game 5 and take Ballard out of the lineup. Rome and partner Salo are both minus-2 for goals scored at even strength. The vaunted Vancouver power play is powerless, blanked in four manpower advantages.

Chicago is starting to look like the Blackhawks of old. Marian Hossa gets his first goal of the series when the Chicago right-winger scores on a power play early in the game with a long, drifting wrist shot that handcuffs Luongo. A few seconds later it's 2–0 when Keith blasts home a shot from the point. The Canucks appear disorganized in the defensive zone. Chicago scores a third goal in the opening period on another power play when Kane makes Luongo look hopeless. The Blackhawks now have six power play goals in the last seven periods. Clearly they have Luongo's number.

Luongo starts the second period as Vigneault allows his starter some leeway. Hossa almost immediately scores on a breakaway and Luongo's night is over as he skates to be bench, carefully tapping Schneider's pads as the goaltenders cross paths during the changeover. Schneider gives up a goal to Keith on another point shot in the third, but at least he stops thirteen of fourteen shots. The Canucks are in disarray after a five-goal humbling before the anxious homefolk, who wonder if their team is capable of regaining its stride. To many observers, this series is looking a lot like the last two playoffs against Chicago as the Blackhawks feed off the leadership of Toews and Keith.

The Canucks have gone from overconfident to having no confidence. Vancouver's top players are no-shows once again. Doubt is creeping in as suddenly the Canucks are looking rather ordinary, especially Luongo, their highest-paid player, earning an estimated $10 million this season. "I've looked up to Roberto for a long time," Crawford says after his thirty-six-save shutout. "To finally be up in this league and playing against him in the playoffs is special." But there was nothing special about Luongo on this night, allowing four goals on twelve shots.

Luongo tries to put a positive spin on things after Game 5, talking about staying composed and being fortunate to have a couple days off so the players can regroup and get back to doing what they do best. "You have to look at the positives in this series," Bieksa says. "You know what? We're still up [three games to two] in the series. We don't want to get too down on ourselves. We look forward to stealing a game in Chicago." Vigneault professes to have "tremendous faith" in his players, even after their response in the fifth game was nothing short of disgusting to most people.

The Blackhawks are playing loose, notes Kane. The Canucks are not. They are tighter than a drum. Vancouver's top line of Burrows with the Sedins produced only five shots on goal in Game 5. Defenceman Edler had the most of any Canuck with five. Clearly the Canucks need a more determined push in the offensive zone. The bottom line here is that Luongo has given up ten goals in two games on just forty shots. The Canucks need their highest-salaried player to be their best player, and he isn't by a long shot.

Chicago backup Turco expresses empathy for Luongo because he's under so much pressure. Luongo's

track record against Chicago is not encouraging, especially the last two springs when the Blackhawks ruled in six games each year. Luongo needs, for his own good, to prove that he can handle a high-flying team like Chicago. The Vancouver talk-radio shows are filled with Luongo talk. Many of the callers want Vigneault to make a goaltending change in midstream, to start the rookie Schneider for the first time in the NHL playoffs. Canuck players put up a bold front in defence of Luongo, their goalie who won thirty-eight games during the regular season and combined with Schneider to earn the Jennings Trophy.

Cory Schneider relieves Luongo in the second period of Game 5 but can't stop the Chicago barrage. RIC ERNST/PNG

Luongo shaves his playoff beard between games and offers that he's definitely ready to be the starter in Game 6 at Chicago. "My confidence is as good as it has been since November," he says. "The way I play is not going to change." When the Canucks get to Chicago, Vigneault lets Schneider know he's the starting net-minder in the sixth game. Luongo will be rested. Some people think Vigneault's job is on the line and he's panicked. Not so, insists the head coach.

"He's just as good as I am and it doesn't matter who's in net," says Luongo without blinking an eye. "It's a team game. Me and Schneids, we had the best goaltending duo all year long. I put the team ahead of myself." There are other lineup changes also for Game 6 as Vigneault goes into his juggling act. Andrew Alberts replaces Rome on defence and fourth-liner Oreskovich comes in for Glass. Chicago gets a boost when Seabrook returns on defence, apparently concussion-free.

In the furious first period of Game 6 the Canucks take the lead twice. Daniel Sedin scores on a wrap-around on Crawford before Chicago evens it on a goal by Bickell, but only after Schneider turns the puck over behind the end red line when attempting a pass. Vancouver goes ahead 2–1 when Burrows scores on a rush after Schneider successfully makes a breakout pass. In the second period Schneider stands tall when the Canucks are two men short after penalties to Torres and Raymond. Schneider gets a lot of help from pen-alty-killers Kesler, Burrows and Hamhuis as they block shot after shot. Chicago manages to tie the score later in the second when Schneider is caught out of the crease, again trying to play the puck, and Bolland scores.

The Canucks have regained some of their confidence, mostly through penalty killing, and are playing like they did earlier in the series. Vancouver takes the lead 3–2 in the third when Bieksa scores on a rebound after a rush by Raymond. This gripping game has many twists and turns as momentum swings back and forth. Later in the third, Hamhuis has difficulty defending a rush and, when trying to recover, trips Frolik, resulting in a penalty shot for the Chicago forward. Schneider can't make the save, the game is tied and Schneider goes down in a heap. He must come out of the game and is replaced by Luongo, whose bench rest ends after forty-two minutes and eighteen seconds.

The game goes to overtime and Luongo stops ten shots before he's eventually beaten at 15:30 on a rebound by Chicago rookie Smith, his third goal of the series. Chicago wins 4–3 and the series is deadlocked at three games each, heading back to Vancouver for one final showdown in Game 7.

"I thought we were the better team," offers Samuelsson. "But you can't say that after you lose." Henrik Sedin chimes in, "They looked tired out there. We took over halfway through the game. If we keep our pace up like we did tonight, we're going to be successful. We battled hard." Yes, they did. The Canucks protected Schneider the best they could and Vigneault's bold gamble nearly paid off, until the fateful penalty shot. Schneider was forced from the game because of leg cramps, something that hindered him earlier in his career, but not in his first full season with the Canucks.

Schneider figures to be healthy enough to play in the deciding seventh game, but there's clearly no reason not to come back with Luongo at Rogers Arena. After all, he won an Olympic gold medal with Canada on home ice at Vancouver in 2010 with an overtime decision over the United States that included a game-saving stop on Joe Pavelski in sudden-death. Luongo has far more experience than Schneider in this type of situation, so even though he allowed the overtime goal to Smith, Vigneault figures to go with his No. 1 goalkeeper. Schneider makes sure he backs up his coach's decision, calling Luongo the "ultimate competitor."

Game 7 against Chicago will be the team's most important game since the spring of 1994 when Vancouver, in the first round of the playoffs, rallied from a 3–1 series deficit against Calgary to beat the Flames three straight on overtime goals by Geoff Courtnall, Trevor Linden and Pavel Bure. The Canucks would reach their second Stanley Cup final that spring, eventually losing in seven games to the New York Rangers in regulation time. Luongo insists this is not the time for the Canucks to feel sorry for themselves after blowing a three-game lead against the Blackhawks. He feels certain the Canucks will roll up their sleeves and get back to work with their season on the line.

Before Game 7, Gillis complains publicly about Chicago getting more power plays than Vancouver when the score is close during the past four games. What he says privately to the league is unclear, but he's convinced there's a discrepancy. "I understand Mike's frustration," Vigneault says in backing his GM. "But as far as us coaches and players, there's nothing we can do about that and we just have to go out and play. We need to be focused on the process, putting a good game on the ice."

Slaying the dragon

Over the years the Canucks have compiled a 5–4 record in Game 7 showdowns, winning their previous seventh game 4–1 in 2007 against the Dallas Stars when Luongo out-duelled Turco. Henrik Sedin played in that game against Dallas and he's learned that teams often use more than one starting goaltender in a series. He reminds inquiring media that Canadian coach Mike Babcock changed goaltenders in the 2010 Olympics, with Luongo replacing Martin Brodeur as the No. 1 starter. "As a player, it's nice to have been there before," says Burrows, a

Mason Raymond, centre, and Ryan Kesler, right, celebrate and Marian Hossa, left, doesn't as Canucks draw first blood in Game Seven of the Western Conference quarter finals.

MARK VAN MANEN/PNG

member of the 2006–7 Canucks. "I remember my first one. I was nervous, wondering what it would be like. My focus [now] is way different than it was back then."

Vigneault is forced into a lineup change because Salo left the previous game in the third period and didn't return after apparently suffering a leg injury. This means Ballard draws back into the lineup as the depth on defence is tested again. This is the first year Ballard has been in the NHL post-season after missing the playoffs during his five seasons with Phoenix and Florida. His last playoffs were in 2001 when he was a teenager with Omaha in the United States Hockey League.

Judgment Day for the Canucks comes on Tuesday, April 26, and the crowd at Rogers Arena is nervous, but loudly enthusiastic when Mark Donnelly sings "O Canada." It doesn't take long for the Canucks to regain their trust as Vancouver scores after only 2:43. Burrows takes a pass from Kesler in the low slot and snaps a shot past Crawford. It's a brilliant rush by Kesler as he slips past defender Keith and sends a perfect backhand pass to Burrows for his second goal of these playoffs. Vigneault has shifted personnel on his top two lines and created a speed line using Kesler between wingers Raymond and Burrows. They play most of their shifts against Chicago captain Toews and his companion Kane.

In the second period the Canucks go into their defensive mode using a one-four forechecking system. Vigneault wants to clog the neutral zone to negate Chicago's speed entering the Vancouver zone. The Sedins and Samuelsson have an overpowering shift in the second, but they are unable to beat Crawford, who turns aside fifteen shots in the middle period. The

Canucks have a chance to put the game away on the first shift of the third period when Burrows is awarded a penalty shot after being pulled down by Keith. He's denied by Crawford at the twenty-one-second mark and Chicago remains within a goal of Vancouver. The Blackhawks give the green light to defencemen Keith and Campbell, allowing them to rush the puck whenever there's open ice. The Canucks are backchecking furiously to help their defence.

The white towels come out as Alex Burrows takes a pass from Ryan Kesler and gives the Canucks a one-goal lead in the first period of Game 7.

MARK VAN MANEN/PNG

Late in the third, after Crawford keeps the Canucks at bay, Keith is penalized for hooking. Vancouver is unable to get the insurance goal as the desperate Blackhawks defend tenaciously. When will Chicago pull Crawford for an extra attacker? There's no need for that strategy because Chicago suddenly strikes for the equalizer at

18:04. The determined Toews shows his leadership while killing the penalty, scoring a shorthanded goal on a rebound after Luongo stopped Hossa. It's a two-against-three rush that produces the first goal of the playoffs by Toews. Tie ballgame, 1–1. Overtime looms.

Both teams are near exhaustion, especially players like Toews, Kesler, Keith and Bieksa, who log so many important minutes. The rest before overtime is welcomed as Game 7 goes to sudden-death. Which team will bend first? The Canucks almost have their season go down the drain early in overtime. The anxiety-riddled crowd is nearly silenced when Burrows is penalized

It's Burrows again as the Canucks eke out a squeaker in overtime of Game 7. MARK VAN MANEN/PNG

for holding after only twenty-four seconds. Chicago's power play is poised to win the game.

Now it's Luongo's turn to show what he's made from. He responds with perhaps his best-ever save in a Canucks uniform, turning back a clean-cut scoring chance by Sharp at the far side of the net after a cross-ice pass by Toews. Luongo's depth in the crease allows him to move post-to-post in the nick of time. The crowd responds instantly with appreciative howls of "Luoooo, Luoooo," cascading to ice level as the Canucks survive a scary moment.

Just over three minutes later the fans are on their feet again. This time it's to cheer as the Canucks win 2–1 in the blink of an eye when Burrows scores an unassisted goal. He more than redeems himself after the penalty. Burrows skates into almost perfect defensive position, just inside the Chicago blue line, and gloves down a high clearance by defender Chris Campoli. The interception gives Burrows a partial breakaway and instantly he hammers a long, high shot into the net, beating Crawford on the blocker glove side at 5:22. Pandemonium breaks out in the Chicago end of the ice as the Canucks pour off the bench in celebration. Burrows slides along the ice on his backside and is buried by rejoicing teammates. The first to get there are linemates Kesler and Raymond before the dogpile grows into a sea of arms and legs.

Burrows scores both Vancouver goals and the Canucks live to play another round in the playoffs. The embattled Luongo responds to

OVERLEAF: The Vancouver Canucks dogpile on the ice as they celebrate Alex Burrows' big overtime goal, finally ending the Blackhawk curse. GERRY KAHRMANN/PNG

criticism with a solid game, with his thirty-second and final save giving the Canucks a chance to win in over-time when they get the break they so desperately need. "It was a great finish," Burrows says with an ever-present smile after the game. "I just want to thank the guys for killing the penalty early in overtime. That's the worst spot to be, in the penalty box. I'm happy Lui made that save off Sharp so I could get back out there and get a shot on net. We believed we could get it done and it felt even better getting it done this way. We told ourselves tonight was our night and we weren't to get outdone by them. It feels good."

During the season and series, many spectators have been taking in a bizarre scene in the stands near the penalty box, where two fans dressed in hideous skin-tight costumes go through attention-getting acrobatics that include handstands and body-presses against the protective glass. The Green Men have become celebrities during the season for their antics intended to distract visiting players in the penalty box. This time the green guys and the legion of Canucks fans have a lot to applaud.

Vigneault also managed to get the attention of his team when he started Schneider in the sixth game. The Canucks followed it with a near-perfect Game 7, with just a couple glitches. "You always say in tough times that's when you see the true character of somebody," says the relieved Luongo. "Obviously it was a big game in my career." Yes, the dragon that is Chicago had been successfully eliminated. The Blackhawks are unable to defend the championship.

Canucks captain Henrik Sedin sums up the series from his perspective by saying he noticed the Blackhawks tiring, leaning over their sticks to get their breath during play stoppages. "We knew if we kept going for another period, they were going to make mistakes," Henrik says. "They had no business being in this series, [but] we made it tough on ourselves." The Canucks had blown a three-game lead before blowing down the Blackhawks on a Burrows blast for the ages. It ranks right up there with Bure's double-overtime goal in Game 7 against Calgary seventeen years earlier. Bring on Nashville is the cry from suddenly confident-again fans.

## CHAPTER FOUR

*"He's just playing lights out and is dragging
people along with him."*
— Mike Gillis praises the efforts
of Ryan Kesler against Nashville.

Finding the Energizer Bunny

The second round of the playoffs has been a falling-off point for the Canucks in their last three trips to the post-season. Vancouver lost to Anaheim in 2007 when Luongo was beaten from far out by Scott Niedermayer in the second overtime period of the fifth game of the Western Conference semifinal. Two years ago the Canucks lost 7–5 in Game 6 at Chicago and last year the Blackhawks prevailed 5–1 in the sixth game in Vancouver. Vancouver and Nashville have never met in the playoffs and Vigneault must plan how to go about the business of matching lines against the Predators' extremely competent defence pairing of Shea Weber and Ryan Suter. They are physical defenders and sure to play mostly against the Sedin brothers, as every team puts out their top defencemen against Daniel and Henrik.

Vigneault went into these playoffs with a post-season coaching record of 17–17 and his biggest battle has

Young Canuck fan displays Ryan Kesler's number to show her appreciation of his heroics during second round action against the Nashville Predators. STUART DAVIS/PNG

been keeping the Vancouver defence from falling apart. Sami Salo has been injured again and Vigneault has moved Aaron Rome, Keith Ballard and Andrew Alberts in and out of the lineup. The workload for Kevin Bieksa, Christian Ehrhoff, Dan Hamhuis and Alexander Edler has been strenuous and the head coach would like to bring a better balance to playing time. The Predators do not have a dominating forward line; they pretty much score by committee. Nashville relies on their top defencemen and the solid netminding of emerging star Pekka Rinne, a brilliant stopper from Finland. Rinne is a finalist for the Vezina Trophy, for the NHL goalkeeper considered the best at his position, along with Luongo and Boston's Tim Thomas.

Hamhuis played six seasons for the Predators before signing with the Canucks last summer and he has a good handle on how Nashville coach Barry Trotz runs his team. The Predators got by Anaheim in the first round behind Rinne and six points from centre Mike Fisher, obtained from Ottawa just before the trade deadline in February. "On paper they may not look like they have as good a team as others, but they're very good," Hamhuis says. "We don't want that to surprise us or fool us. They had ninety-nine points and they're in the second round for a reason." Vancouver and Nashville split four games during the regular season when Rinne had a miniscule 1.26 goals-against average against the Canucks.

Canucks winger Chris Higgins promises there will be no "emotional hangovers" after the tough Chicago series, noting that Nashville is a dangerous team with a lot of "good components." Those elements include two scoring lines. Fisher centres a unit with wingers Sergei

Kostitsyn and Patric Hornqvist, with Dave Legwand the middleman on another line with Joel Ward and Martin Erat. Legwand is the longest-serving Nashville player. He was a first-round draft pick in 1998, the year the Predators entered the NHL through expansion, and is appearing in his fifth Stanley Cup playoffs. He's played more games and scored more goals than anyone in franchise history. The Canucks figure Legwand will play as much as any Nashville forward this series because he's also skilled at taking draws, which means he'll probably see a lot of Kesler in the faceoff circle.

Vigneault is never quite sure of the makeup of his first three lines because of his penchant for switching around wingers. But he has depth up front, much more than Nashville, with Alex Burrows, Mikael Samuelsson and Jannik Hansen all capable of playing right wing on any of the top units. If there's one worry for Vigneault and his staff, it's the inconsistency of the Vancouver offence. Goals are getting harder to come by because everyone preaches a defence-first attitude in the playoffs.

In Game 1 against Nashville, the Canucks show great energy in the first period at Rogers Arena. Vigneault sticks with the same forwards who played the last game against Chicago. He makes a change on defence, with Rome replacing Alberts. Vancouver outshoots the Predators 16–5 in the scoreless opening period, held at bay by the 6-foot-5 Rinne. He's as good as advertised. He flashes the leather, snagging many a shot with his gloved left hand.

The Canucks keep pushing in the second and just past the midway point they're rewarded by their third line. Newcomers Maxim Lapierre and Higgins are flying,

along with Hansen. Their work pays dividends when Higgins scores on a setup by Lapierre. The puck goes in and out of the net so fast off the back bar that a video review is needed to confirm it's a goal. "I just kind of loaded up," Higgins says, "and managed to get it in there. You always want to get another one, but it was that kind of game. There weren't a lot of scoring chances."

Luongo gets the 1–0 shutout by stopping twenty shots, including nine in the third period. He's lucky when Weber misfires late in the game during a Nashville power play with Ballard in the penalty box for holding. Earlier in the game, Ballard infuriated the Predators with a hip check that sent rough-and-tumble Nashville winger Jordin Tootoo cartwheeling with his skates passing over Ballard's head. Still, the Canucks hang on at the end of game and need a late faceoff win by Kesler and a blocked shot by Henrik Sedin to come away winners.

After the game, Vancouver players insist they didn't have a letdown against Nashville, a team that finished fifth in the Western Conference standings. The Predators are everything people feared, namely a club capable of playing solid team defence. "If they keep the game tight, that's where they want to be," says Henrik Sedin. "But there's a chance they can get on us if we start running around frustrated and cheating a bit, going into third periods trying to get goals. We can't do that." Daniel Sedin agrees with his twin brother: "This is what we expect, 1–0, 2–1 games. We have to be ready for that."

So after all the excitement of

Chris Higgins 20 and Max Lapierre celebrate the only goal in a 1–0 victory over the Nashville Predators to start the series. MARK VAN MANEN/PNG

91

the Chicago series, playing Nashville means scoring on the odd opportunity while playing airtight defence. The Canucks may not like this approach, but realize what's in store for them. "Goalies have won series before and we have to get second-chance opportunities," Higgins says about the problem Rinne presents.

Another issue after the game is the low check by Ballard on Tootoo, with the Vancouver player penalized for clipping. Ballard doesn't agree and replays show it was a hip-high check delivered to the body of Tootoo rather than at knee level. After being a healthy scratch twice in the Chicago series, Ballard had an overall strong game against Nashville while playing eleven minutes and twelve seconds. "You have to play a little bit on that edge," Ballard says about his penchant for throwing hip checks. "If you're a physical player, you have to be physical and that's an area where I can contribute. If I went too low, that's for me to adjust."

This series pits two of the three finalists for the Jack Adams Award given to the NHL coach of the year. Vigneault, Trotz and Pittsburgh's Dan Bylsma have been nominated, Vigneault for the third time. He won in 2007, his first season with the Canucks. Nashville defenceman Shane O'Brien has played for both Trotz and Vigneault. O'Brien was in Vigneault's doghouse last season over conditioning levels and the Canucks moved the robust O'Brien to the Predators just before the start of this season in a trade for depth defenceman Ryan Parent, who spent almost the entire season in the minors with the Manitoba Moose. "A.V. has a little bit more firepower up front than Trotzy has to work with, so Trotzy's more of a defensive-minded guy," O'Brien says in analyzing the two bench bosses. "But you gotta give A.V. tons of credit. Talent alone doesn't win hockey games."

Between Games 1 and 2, Vigneault frets about his power play, which hasn't scored on fourteen manpower advantages over the last four games. But he's careful not to be overly critical of his star players who eat up much of the power-play time. "The way we're playing it," explains Vigneault, "the way we were retrieving pucks, the way we were moving it around makes for a power play that should have some success. It didn't [in the opener], but it did everything it was supposed to do except score." Vigneault wants Kesler to stay in front of the net on the power play. Kesler expects to take a pounding from Suter and Weber while attempting to screen Rinne.

Rogers Arena is jumping before Game 2, especially when Elvis Costello makes a brief appearance with the Canucks' house band, the Odds, including a lively rendition of "Pump It Up." After a scoreless first period, the Canucks get the lead they want early in the second when Burrows scores shorthanded on a pass from Kesler, with Ehrhoff in the penalty box for tripping. Then the Canucks go into a defensive mode that proves costly as they lose their initiative to attack the Nashville goal. "We were on our heels," Bieksa says later. "We couldn't get the puck off the wall. We were hemmed in our zone for shifts at a time. It's hard to get shots on goal when you are always hemmed in our own end."

The Predators attack relentlessly and are rewarded late in the third period when Suter joins a Nashville rush and ends up deep in the Vancouver zone. Suter moves out a step toward the goal area and fires a desperation shot into traffic. The puck bounces off Luongo's skate and in the confusing scramble Luongo inadvertently kicks the puck into his own net with sixty-seven seconds left in regulation. Tie game, and overtime looms. "It hit the heel of my stick and hit my [skate] heel and went in," Luongo explains about why he's allowed unexpected goals late in play-off games. "Sometimes it happens. Obviously you try not to give up a goal late."

The Canucks play reasonably

Ryan Kesler can't solve Predator netminder Pekka Rinne, who was in top form for Game

2. IAN LINDSAY/PNG

well in the first overtime period, but are denied eleven times by Rinne, who is at the top of his game, especially on a dangerous shot by Bieksa from the side of the net. Vancouver is still outshooting Nashville in the second overtime, 6–3, when the game abruptly ends. The Predators tie the series 1–1 when Matt Halischuk picks the top corner on Luongo's glove side at 14:51 for the sudden-death decision. It's a shot many critics thought Luongo should stop, but it's delivered quickly and decisively by Halischuk on a counterattack rush after Rome was trapped up ice. The Canucks have another solid defensive game, but Rinne has played almost lights-out. He makes forty-five saves, while Luongo did not look particularly confident on either goal in the 2–1 defeat.

Nashville players wanted to change the mood of the series and Halischuk was sure they did just that in Game 2, giving the Predators the momentum heading into the next two games in Nashville. "We talked about being resilient and we've been that this year," says Halischuk, who in 2008 scored the overtime winner for Canada that gave the national junior team a world championship.

In the Canucks dressing room, Luongo puts his spin in the series by saying it is tightly played and that he anticipates more overtimes because there is little space for creativity. "There's not going to be a lot of room for mistakes," he adds. It's a red flag for Vancouver. The Sedins aren't scoring and neither is Samuelsson. The Canucks definitely have a problem, insiders agree. In the last nine games, Vancouver has scored just eighteen goals. "We've been through this a lot and we know we have to score more," says Daniel Sedin as he faces the inquiring media. "We need to get more shots and grind it out. There's not going to be a lot of high-scoring games." Both Sedins deny they're injured, though neither has played with much energy. The physicality of the Predators, especially Weber and Suter, appears to be having an effect on top Canuck players.

Vigneault understands what's happening and late in Game 2 switches Burrows back to the Sedin line and drops Samuelsson all the way to the third unit. Give the Canuck coach credit for making adjustments, though sometimes he's a little late in making up his mind. Vigneault looks at the playoff scoring stats between games. He sees the Canucks have scored three goals only three times in these playoffs. This output from the team that led the league in goal scoring in the regular season? He tries to understand why. So do the Sedins. "We know when we're playing our best, we're playing fast-paced hockey," Henrik says. "That comes with short shifts and getting pucks to where we want to forecheck. [Last game] they were the team that had the higher pace."

The Vancouver power play has drawn a blank against Nashville. The Canucks have misfired six times in two games. Samuelsson, a winger who gets playing time at the point on one of the power-play units, is mystified. "It feels like we're getting chances," Samuelsson says, "but we've got to bury them. We've got to figure that one out." Samuelsson has not played particularly well during the post-season. His ice time is cut back as he seems to be labouring with his stride. His regular-season numbers were down also, to eighteen goals from thirty the previous year. "It really hasn't gone my way," says Samuelsson, who studies the game intently. "I'm trying

Former teammates Ryan Kesler and Shane O'Brien get reacquainted in front of the Predators' net. LES BAZSO/PNG

to work a little harder. Hopefully it will come." During practice before Game 3, Vigneault drops Samuelsson to the fourth line, where he skates with rookie Cody Hodgson and Tanner Glass.

Meantime, there's a definite buzz in Nashville as the country music stronghold known as Music City braces for a further taste of playoff hockey. The Predators have missed the post-season only once in the past eight years, but they've also won only one opening-round series, against Anaheim. Singing star Carrie Underwood, wife of Predators centre Mike Fisher, watches nearly every game at Bridgestone Arena. Nashville general manager David Poile, who is the son of Norman "Bud" Poile, the first NHL GM for the Canucks, figures Nashville has truly become a hockey hotbed after starting out as a non-traditional market. Fisher says his wife is excited about the Predators' chances and Underwood is in her usual seat for Game 3, anxious to see how her husband fares against Kesler. Even the Green Men have travelled to Nashville to exhibit their costumes as they cheer for the visiting Canucks.

The crowd likes what they see as the Predators storm into the lead when Legwand scores a shorthanded goal midway through the first period after a turnover by Edler. Luongo keeps the score close with a save on Steve Sullivan, who had broken into the clear. Hamhuis is trying to do too much and must settle down as he plays before many of the fans who once cheered him. The Canucks pull even in the second period when Kesler scores on the power play, converting a pass in the blue-iced crease from Ehrhoff that gave Kesler an open net to hit. Vancouver soon begins to get an edge in possession, though the defensive pairing of Edler and Rome struggles.

Vancouver goes ahead 2–1 early in the third when Higgins shows his patience on a rush with Kesler. Higgins stays with the play, circles the net and scores from the right circle as Rinne scrambles too late to get back in position. Nashville doesn't back off, though, and is rewarded

Kesler gets a rare puck past Vezina candidate Pekka Rinne, who stood on his head to frustrate Canuck shooters. JENELLE SCHNEIDER/PNG

when Ward ties the score at 13:18 with a rather soft goal following an Ehrhoff turnover that left Alberts alone to defend in front of Luongo. Overtime looms again.

The Canucks get a break in overtime when Weber is called for hooking. Samuelsson is pressed into action at the left point and unloads a shot that Kesler deftly tips into the net for the winning goal, making the final score 3–2. Vancouver leads the series 2–1.

Vancouver plays much better offensively this game with forty-seven shots on Rinne, but still scores only three times. The Sedins look better playing with Burrows on their wing than they did with Samuelsson or Hansen. Kesler's three points are the biggest difference as secondary scoring emerges. "I put the same game on the ice, but I finally got the results," Kesler says. "I didn't lack in confidence. I never thought for once I couldn't score. I didn't change my game at all." Bieksa appreciates the diligent work by one of his best friends on the team. "He's leading the way out there. It's about time he got rewarded for his hard work. You're not going to keep him off the score sheet for very long."

The Predators complain about the penalty on Weber, insisting Kesler is holding onto Weber's stick when the call is made. But that's playoff hockey, when only a few of the infractions are actually called. The Canucks get a break and Vigneault is rewarded for making changes that made a difference. Bieksa provides an honest evaluation of his team when he says the Canucks must bear down and keep their nose to the grindstone, especially late in the third period. "Those last few minutes are crucial," he says. "We're not going to go far if we're letting in goals in the last five minutes." The Canucks are trying to match the physicality of the Predators, who take their lead from team captain Weber. Vancouver is getting more bodychecks from Alberts, who leads the team with five hits in the third game. Alberts is not a graceful skater, but at 6-foot-5 provides an obstacle in the defensive zone.

Vigneault goes out of his way to praise the Kesler line before Game 4. The coach really likes the speed of Kesler, Higgins and Raymond. They manage to back off the Nashville defence, giving the Canucks space to enter the offensive zone. "That whole line was real strong," Vigneault points out. "Higgins played one of his best games since he's been with us."

Rinne uses his full 6'5" to snuff a dangerous break by Alex Burrows in Game 5. JENELLE SCHNEIDER/PNG

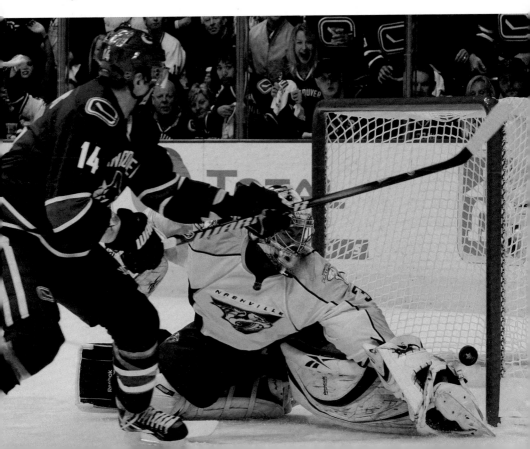

Kesler and Burrows continue their effectiveness killing penalties, forcing the Predators to the outside through neutral ice. "Winning the special teams battles is what's going to win games at this time of year," Kesler says.

There's still concern in the Vancouver camp about the production, or lack of it, by the Sedins. They've been outscored by Ward, a checker. Vigneault is quick to defend his offensive stars. "Maybe they didn't get on the score sheet [in Game 3], but they spent some quality time in the other team's end doing what they do," Vigneault says about the Sedins and their offensive-zone cycle tendencies. "I'm confident with the effort they showed. They'll be rewarded soon." Also of concern is the performance of Ballard on defence. His inconsistency gives the coaching staff second thoughts about dressing him next game in Nashville. Ballard claims he hasn't lost confidence, but his play indicates otherwise.

Vigneault and his coaches like what they see in other areas of the Vancouver game, especially on the second and third lines. Kesler's line is scoring again, while Lapierre has fit in nicely on the third line between wingers Raffi Torres and Hansen, right in the position once occupied by the injured Manny Malhotra. Higgins and Lapierre, the late-season acquisitions, appear to be relishing the intensity of the playoffs. "These guys worked so hard all year to finish first, you don't want to be the guys who come in and ruin it," says Lapierre. "So we had to step up our game." The team also gets a boost when defenceman Sami Salo returns from injury to resume regular duty. His experience is invaluable.

The Sedins don't seem to have their skating legs early in the fourth game and get hemmed in the defensive zone. The Canucks hold the fort and the Sedins start to play at the tempo they desire. Henrik and Daniel assist on a goal by Ehrhoff in the first period, with Burrows providing the screen in front of Rinne. The Predators don't buckle as Ward continues his scoring with a power-play marker late in the first after Salo was penalized for delay of game when he cleared the puck into the stands from the defensive zone.

The Canucks forge a 2–1 lead in the second period when Edler scores from the point, with Rinne's vision hampered by his own defenders in front of the net. Again, Nashville refuses to fold, stubbornly staying in the game. Nashville pulls even in the third when defenceman Cody Franson, the one-time Vancouver Giants junior, scores from the point with a shot that goes between Luongo's leg pads. On this shift the fourth line of the Predators was better than the fourth unit of the Canucks.

Once again, though, it is Kesler to the rescue as he scores a brilliant goal on the rush during a power play. Kesler takes a pass from Henrik Sedin in neutral ice and hits the Nashville blue line with speed, backing in defenders Shane O'Brien and Kevin Klein. Kesler stays on his forehand and works his way between the lunging defenders, using his speed to advantage. Kesler scores the winning goal at 7:28 with a wicked wrist shot that's virtually unstoppable. The Canucks add an insurance marker for the 4–2 final when Henrik Sedin scores into an unguarded net after Rinne is pulled for an extra attacker. Sedin started the play by winning a faceoff from Fisher in the Vancouver zone.

One of the keys to Game 4 was the ability of the Vancouver penalty killers to shine during a two-man disadvantage in the second period after Lapierre went off for interference and Rome for slashing, leaving the Canucks two skaters short for forty-seven seconds. The other key was Kesler, as he's taken over the series. "It wasn't a set play at all," Kesler says about his winning goal. "I just freelanced. It was a great play by Hank [Sedin] to hit me in stride." Kesler has spent countless hours in the off-season perfecting his wrist shot. He also shoots in the team gym between games at home. "It's an amazing play by a player whose will to win right now is very strong," offers Vigneault.

Trying to pass around the credit for a 3–1 series lead, Kesler again talks about the resiliency of the Canucks and the push-back after giving up a second goal to the Predators. Ehrhoff credits a tip from the injured Malhotra for his goal. "Manny said, 'Just get a nice wrister on net,'" explains Ehrhoff. "I didn't have enough time to slap it, so it worked out fine. [Malhotra's] around and helping the guys out and keeping the guys motivated. He saw this as a must-win for us. Now we've got to try and close it out."

Bieksa likes the way the Canucks have become so serious during two road games, noting any shift can help determine the outcome of a game. "Everyone takes that to heart," he says. "[Nashville is] going to try to beat us by outworking us. We're going to have to counter with our work ethic and letting our skill take over." Burrows notes that a lot of little things go unnoticed—blocked shots and backchecking, for example—but those are the things that win close games in playoffs. The Canucks had three chances to put away Chicago in the opening round and now they can eliminate Nashville in Game 5 at Rogers Arena. Or will they?

Vancouver takes a 2–1 lead in the fifth game on goals by Torres and Kesler in the first period after Legwand opens the scoring for Nashville. The Canucks are on their game, but Luongo isn't in top form, it turns

Third liners Raffi Torres and Maxim Lapierre continue to fly as Torres scores in Game 5, but the Predators battle back. LES BAZSO/PNG

out. The Canucks lose Samuelsson to injury in the first period and the game starts to swing in Nashville's direction. The Predators pull into a 2–2 deadlock in the second on an unassisted marker by Legwand, his second goal of the game. The shifty Ward puts the game away in the third with two goals and Nashville hangs on to win 4–3 after Kesler scores his second of the game at 15:14 of the third.

Luongo faces only twenty-three shots and is beaten four times, while Bieksa commits a turnover on the go-ahead goal. As bad as that was, Edler was worse, constantly getting into trouble defensively. Plus, Henrik Sedin lost two faceoffs to Fisher after Vancouver pulled Luongo for an extra skater in the last minute. The Canucks have too much dead weight in the lineup, sending the series back to Nashville.

"We need to play better," Daniel Sedin admits. "We can't rely on Kesler's line only. I was minus-four and that can't happen. It's unacceptable. We need to score on our chances. It's the same old story." Vigneault talks about it being a "game of mistakes" and the Canucks certainly made their share of miscues on this occasion.

Blue-line breakdowns are one thing, but letting a checker like Ward dominate is mindboggling. Ward scored ten goals during the regular season and now has seven in the playoffs—not bad for a journeyman heading toward unrestricted free agency. Nashville coach Trotz has instructed his team to go for it. No more sitting back and waiting. "The guys responded," says Trotz. "I'll take a page out of Tampa Bay and [former coach] John Tortorella: 'Safe is death and we didn't play safe. We played to win tonight and got rewarded.'"

There are no rewards for the Canucks when they make so many glaring errors near Luongo and the Vancouver net. Edler just wants to put the game behind him and get ready for Game 6. "There's no easy game against these guys," concedes Edler. "It's not like we played in the fifth game against Chicago [the Canucks lost 5–0 on home ice]. We've got to look ahead to the next game." Hamhuis agrees. "Hopefully we've learned our lesson," Hamhuis sighs. "We won't want to extend it."

There are three definite standouts in the Nashville series: Kesler for the Canucks with eleven points in five games, plus Ward and Rinne. Ward has ignited the Predator offence with his finish around the net, scoring four times in the series, and Rinne has made numerous spectacular saves. Trotz has been able to use his fourth line extensively as the unit of Nick Spaling, Halischuk and Jerred Smithson has been better than any combination of fourth liners iced by Vigneault.

The Canucks definitely need the Sedins to show some finish around the net. They have dominated at times with their puck possession, but need to put shots on net with greater frequency. Vigneault opines that the negative plus-minus rating of the Sedins is an unfair statistic. "They couldn't do anything about Edler putting the puck into our net," Vigneault says about one of the Nashville goals the previous game. "They couldn't do anything on the Samuelsson turnover [leading to another goal] and they couldn't do anything on the other two turnovers. They're working extremely well and hard and I'm supporting them 100 percent. The points are going to come." Daniel Sedin insists the twins will bounce back, just like they did in the Chicago series. "We can't get frustrated," Daniel suggests before Game 6. "We know it's going to be a tight game."

One thing is definite and that is that Samuelsson is out of the lineup, perhaps for the rest of the play-offs, with an undisclosed lower body injury. Oreskovich is ready to step in. The bruising winger acquired from Florida in the Ballard trade the previous summer is a decent skater who likes to throw his body around on the forecheck. He's not overly effective with the puck, so his minutes are limited, mostly playing against the third and fourth lines. "They've got some defencemen who are playing big minutes," Oreskovich notes. "So I'm going to try to wear them down every time I'm out there." The Canucks want to limit their turnovers against Nashville, with the coaching staff stressing puck possession and percentage passes. "If we limit our mistakes, I think we can limit their offence," says Glass. "When they score four goals on you, it's likely because you turned the puck over or made mistakes."

The Predators are in an upbeat mood before Game 6 because they've erased doubts by extending the series. They feel they're in control of their destiny now, instead of doubting themselves. Resiliency is Nashville's DNA, says coach Trotz. "One of the things we've had in Nashville from day one is, 'Let's not make excuses for anything,'" Trotz says. "And, we don't."

Vigneault makes one lineup change for Game 6. It's not Oreskovich who replaces Samuelsson. It's winger Jeff Tambellini dressing for his first NHL playoff game after missing the post-season when he was with the New York Islanders. Tambellini dressed for sixty-two Canuck games in the regular season and scored nine goals. But he hasn't produced a goal since December 28 against Philadelphia. Vigneault has rolled the dice, knowing Tambellini is more of a threat to score than Oreskovich.

The Predators roll out country music legend Charlie Daniels to sing "The Star Spangled Banner," but the Canucks don't seem to notice. They have a singular focus that shows when Kesler bumps into Rinne— "accidentally on purpose," it looks like—early in the first period. Kesler has been in on eleven of the fourteen Vancouver goals in the series. Luongo seems back on top of his game, stopping all eleven Nashville shots in the first period and the confident Canucks go on the offensive, scoring twice on just seven shots.

Raymond opens the scoring by converting a pass from Kesler. Raymond uses skill and patience as he works his way around Rinne to score on a backhander. Less than two minutes later, the Canucks are on the scoreboard again. Vancouver gets a power-play goal from Daniel Sedin, this time on a pass from the corner by Kesler. Who else would it be? Kesler has thirteen points against the Predators. Nashville is shorthanded after Tootoo was assessed a controversial diving penalty. Still in the first, Tambellini shows why he's in the lineup and validates Vigneault's coaching decision. Erat gets a breakaway from the centre red line and Tambellini instinctively backchecks, using his exceptional speed to catch the Nashville player and bump him off the puck, preventing a clear-cut scoring chance.

The Predators get back in the game in the second period when the persistent Legwand scores with a bank shot from behind the end goal line. Luongo doesn't think the puck went into the net on his short side, but video replays indicate otherwise. The Canucks are outshot 18–9 over two periods, but get their game back in order in the third. Vancouver holds Nashville to six shots on Luongo and manages to kill off a late penalty to Torres.

Raymond's first goal of the playoffs and Daniel Sedin's first of the series give the Canucks a 2–1 decision over Nashville and a 4–2 series win. The defensive pairing of Bieksa and Hamhuis has held Fisher to one point in six games and none for his linemates, Kostitsyn

and Hornqvist. And, in the sixth game, the Canucks were perfect on the penalty kill when they were short-handed four times in the first period and on six occasions overall.

After the series, both head coaches praise Kesler for his leadership and dominance. "He's obviously decided to drive the bus," Vigneault states. "He was our dominant force. We needed that performance—and we need it to continue. We need some other guys to come on board." Trotz took time to speak for a moment with Kesler as they passed each other during the traditional shaking of hands at the end of a series. "I said to him when I went by out there, 'If you don't play like that, we're going to a Game 7 and maybe we win the series,'" Trotz recalls later. "He was a force the whole series. We used multiple people against him. But he played to a level that few people can reach. He just had one of those series, the most incredible six games that we'll probably see."

Kesler took thirty-three shifts in Game 6 and played twenty-two minutes and fifty-four seconds, with an average shift of forty-one seconds. Vigneault wouldn't have wanted it any other way. The coach also found decent linemates for Kesler in this series, using mostly Higgins and Raymond on the wings. Higgins played the last two games on a sore left foot after blocking a shot. He doesn't think he skated that well, preferring to praise teammates.

In a corner of the Vancouver dressing room, Tambellini beams

"The most incredible six games we'll probably see," is how coach Barry Trotz describes Ryan Kesler's dominant series against the Preds. Kes was in on 11 of 14 goals to put Nashville away in six. JENELLE SCHNEIDER/ PNG

about his first NHL playoff game, proud that he has chased down Erat from behind. Known mostly for his offensive skills, Tambellini has contributed defensively. "It was panic right away because I saw a guy with about a zone on me," Tambellini says in recalling his play in the first period. "I just tried to take off and got a good line on the man and was able to separate him. The first playoff game was pretty special and for it to come in an elimination game and be shaking hands afterward was fantastic." Bieksa chimes in, "I imagine tomorrow we'll wake up and it will feel even better."

## CHAPTER FIVE

"You work all your life for the opportunity, all the ups and downs. Now to be able to battle for the Stanley Cup, that's a pretty good feeling."
—Alex Burrows following the San Jose series

A carom for the ages

Ryan Kesler has gained league-wide attention with his two-way play against Nashville and his name begins to be mentioned in discussions about players in the running for the Conn Smythe Trophy as the NHL's most valuable player in the playoffs. Teammates are genuinely enthused about Kesler and praise his leadership. "The guy just doesn't get tired," says Jeff Tambellini. "It doesn't matter if you double-shift him. This guy has stamina like I have never ever seen. It's fun to watch." Alex Burrows played with Kesler in the minors during the lockout season in 2004–05 when Kesler was a twenty-year-old pro rookie. "Now he's more mature," observes Burrows. "He wants to be our guy that leads us to the Promised Land. We're just going to jump on his back and keep going."

Meanwhile, as the Vancouver coaching staff prepares for round three and the San Jose Sharks, there's growing concern the Canucks aren't playing well enough offensively in the Western Conference playoffs. The Canucks need more balance to their attack and that means production from the Sedins and linemate Burrows. "We would like to have more looks offensively," Burrows says. "It's nice to get this far, but we're shooting for more."

Kesler sports some obvious wounds from the Nashville series. He has a scar on his jawline, a swollen mouth and an over-sized nose, all leftovers from his amazing battle with the Predators over six games in which he admirably persevered. He's a man of few words, letting on-ice actions do his talking. "He's been unbelievable," goaltender

Fan Mark Heartwell revs up some support for the Canucks during the Western Conference Finals. GERRY KAHRMANN/PNG

Roberto Luongo says. "He has taken his game to a level that I've never seen before in the second round. He's probably one of the most dominant players in the league right now."

Kesler has amassed fifteen points in thirteen play-off games and understands players don't get a crack at a Stanley Cup championship every day. He's living his dream and enjoying every moment. He credits his father, Mike, for instilling a strong work ethic that carried over into adulthood to where he's now one of the cornerstones of the Vancouver franchise.

Canucks general manager Mike Gillis wants his team to get to an emotional level where players can keep forging ahead, no matter what happens. He wants the Canucks to push through whatever adversities they will face against San Jose, a team with big forwards, but lack of overall size on defence. The Canucks have some time between series to work on a few areas of their game, including the power play.

"Throughout the whole playoffs you need to keep getting better," Kesler says. "Every game, every shift, every minute means something. We're not going to be completely satisfied if we only make it to the third round. We've got to continue to have that will and drive, and I know we do." That's music to the ears of Gillis and head coach Alain Vigneault as the stage is set for a showdown with the Sharks. Vigneault reinforces the facts of life for everyone in noting the significance of continued progress.

"My right-hand man Rick [Bowness, associate coach] was telling me that twenty years ago with the Boston Bruins he made it to the final four," Vigneault says. "It took him twenty years to get back. It's not easy to get here. And when you get here, bust a gut. He got fired that year... after making the final four. So I'm telling you, we're going to bust a gut." The Moncton-born Bowness is in his mid-fifties now and has only one ambition left in hockey and that's to win a Stanley Cup championship. He knows this may be his last chance because opportunity knocks ever so seldom.

When it's suggested to Vigneault, who is from Gatineau, Quebec, that the Canucks should now be considered "Canada's team" as the lone Canadian franchise in the final four, Vigneault wonders if the team has been fully embraced by the rest of the country. "I thought we did have Canada's heart, but I'm hearing rumbles all over the place that we don't have it right now," he says. "I know we have BC's heart. We've got great fans here. They're understanding and supportive, and we're really striving to give them what they want because we want it just as much."

The Canucks have several days off between series and most of the players rest. Tambellini goes for a voluntary workout one day and has a surprise skating partner in Manny Malhotra. The injured centre is back on the ice wearing a full facial shield to protect his injured eye. It will take some kind of miracle to get Malhotra back in uniform again this season, the Canucks suggest, but you never know about the recovery rate of strong-willed athletes. The Sedins are well rested going into the San Jose series, where they figure to get more skating room. This time they're likely to face the defensive duo of Douglas Murray and Dan Boyle. Murray is a hulking 240-pounder who throws heavy bodychecks, while Boyle is much

To take the Western Conference the Canucks would have to get by Antti Niemi, the goalie who ended their 2010 playoff hopes in Chicago. IAN LINDSAY/PNG

smaller and slicker, a puck mover with the skating ability to recover defensively.

"We know we're going to get criticized if we don't score, doesn't matter who we're facing," says Henrik Sedin. "[But] I think I like our matchup against any team. We've got a good team here. That's the way we feel." The Canucks didn't lose a game in regulation against San Jose in four meetings. Vancouver won three times and got a point in the other game when the Sharks won in overtime late in the schedule.

Bieksa and Hamhuis anticipate seeing a lot of Joe Thornton and Patrick Marleau this series, along with Devin Setoguchi. The Sharks also have a dangerous second line with rookie Logan Couture playing between jumbo-sized wingers Ryane Clowe and Dany Heatley. Sharks coach Todd McLellan has an ace in the hole in third-line centre Joe Pavelski, who gets extra duty at the point alongside Boyle on power plays. (It was Pavelski, playing for the United States, who forced Luongo to make a brilliant save in overtime when Canada won the Olympic gold in 2010.) Vigneault keeps his strategy under wraps before the series, though it's expected he'll match Kesler against Thornton whenever possible.

In the much-anticipated opener at Rogers Arena, with far more pre-game hype than in the Nashville series, Thornton gets the only goal in the first period, a gift of sorts when Luongo turns the puck over while trying to make a clearance. The Canucks pull even in the second period as Maxim Lapierre converts a pass from Jannik Hansen after a weak, one-handed clearing attempt by Sharks netminder Antti Niemi. San Jose goes ahead again later in the second on a power play when Marleau neatly tips in a wrist shot by Boyle following an offensive zone penalty to Mason Raymond.

Vancouver is getting a timely lift from its third line of Raffi Torres with Lapierre and Hansen and that seems to energize everyone, including the Sedin line. Bieksa scores the tying goal in the third period when he trails a rush. He's spotted by Burrows, who smartly feeds a pass for Bieksa to snap home a huge goal at 7:02 of the third, with a second assist to Henrik Sedin. That seems to inspire the No. 1 unit and Henrik gets the game-winner seventy-nine seconds later on a power play. Kesler wins a faceoff, point man Christian Ehrhoff spots Henrik in the open and feeds a pass to the captain, who catches Niemi moving the wrong way and deposits the deciding goal in a 3–2 victory. "It's tough to come back in this league," Henrik says later. "We made a great push and showed a lot of courage in the third."

The Canucks are the well-rested team in the opener as the Sharks had little time to prepare after a seven-game marathon with the Detroit Red Wings in the second round. Vancouver had success with defencemen skating up into the rush to create odd-man situations, like Bieksa did on the tying goal. "We have six guys who can jump into the play and we feel we can do it by committee," Bieksa analyzes. "It was the right time. We felt we were wearing them down." Also notable in the Vancouver performance was the play of Daniel Sedin, even though he went pointless. He slid along the ice to block a potentially dangerous shot by Ian White in the third period, then won a late faceoff when the Canucks were caught without a centreman on the ice following an icing, meaning they couldn't change lines and get Kesler to handle the draw.

The Canucks have much to be thankful for after Game 1, especially the contributions of the third line when the team was trailing. Torres plays twenty-two shifts, Hansen twenty-five and Lapierre twenty-three, all around the fifteen-minute mark in ice time and all are plus-one for goals scored at even strength. Much of the time the trio skates in the San Jose zone, keeping possession of the puck. "It was crazy, eh?" beams Torres. "That's the most our line has had the puck in the past five games combined."

The Lapierre line figures in the winning goal, even though they weren't on the ice when Henrik Sedin scores. San Jose winger Heatley gets a penalty for elbowing Torres, who doesn't retaliate, giving Vancouver a power play right after the Bieksa tying marker. "Those guys were unbelievable," Kesler says. "They play in the offensive zone all night [and] it wears the [other team's] D down and makes them really hard to play against." Lapierre explains the line's success saying, "We try to keep it simple: put the puck deep and cycle."

About the only negative in the opener was another gaffe by Luongo, this time on the opening goal by Thornton. It's getting to be a rough ride for the goaltender who some believe has been one of the best performers in the playoffs. "I could hear the fans were a little nervous at times," Luongo admits before adding, "I've done a great job all year [clearing the puck] and don't think it's a weakness in my game."

There's plenty of talk between games about the brewing rivalry between Kesler and Thornton. The San

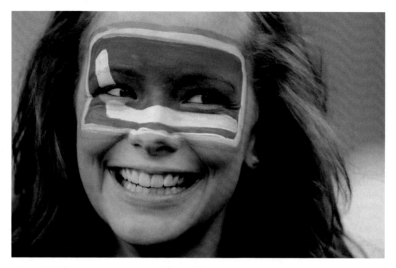

Canucks fan Vanessa Houweling likes what she sees in Game 1. GERRY KAHRMANN/PNG

Jose captain challenged Kesler to a fight a split second after the puck dropped to begin the series. Kesler wisely declined, giving up way too much in size to the 6-foot-4, 230-pound Thornton. "He was asking me to fight, I laughed at him," Kesler explains the next day. "I'm not intimidated by him. I'm not going to be. He's a good player, but no one scares me on the ice." The Canucks need Kesler out of the penalty box. It's the self-control Vigneault has stressed from the start of the season. Kesler insists he has no past history with Thornton, although Kesler is known throughout the Western Conference as a player who gets under the skin of opposing players. "Those guys [like Thornton] are at the top of their class and I want to be better than them every shift, every game," says Kesler. "That's what motivates me."

Sharks coach McLellan talks before Game 2 about what it takes to be successful in playoffs. "You can have all the skill, but if you're not prepared and committed to do it harder and longer than the other team, they'll win out," he says. "Once that skill decides it's going to really compete hard, it doesn't guarantee you a win, but it sure gives you a better chance." McLellan doesn't name what players he wants more from, but it's obvious that the Sharks need high-priced winger Heatley to step up his game. He played twenty-eight shifts in the opener and produced only two shots on goal, with another blocked by the Vancouver defence.

There's concern on talk-radio shows about Luongo and his penchant for allowing soft goals, even though his playoff record is 9–5 this year, with a goals-against average of 2.23. He was marginally better than Niemi in the opener, getting the best of a player who won a Cup ring last year with Chicago. "He never really gets a fair shake in this city and this league," says Cory Schneider in defence of his teammate. "If we win, it's not because of him and if we lose, it's his fault it seems. But he's ignored all the criticism and all the questions. I don't know what more people want from him."

One player the fans have taken a liking to is Lapierre, the late-season acquisition from Anaheim, even after he was assessed a penalty for diving in the opener against the Sharks. It probably was a reputation call from his time spent with the Montreal Canadiens when he was a vocal irritant. "Max has got the reputation of being a rat and he's not well liked on the ice by a lot of guys," says teammate Chris Higgins, who played with Lapierre in Montreal. "But in the locker room, he gets along well." It turns out Lapierre was recommended to the Canucks by the team's eastern pro scout, Lucien DeBlois, and assistant general manager Lorne Henning. Lapierre scored on his only shot in the opener and was not scored against.

Malhotra turns thirty-one and continues to skate with teammates in practice, with wild media speculation about a possible return. Gillis thinks it is "miraculous"

Sami Salo celebrates his first goal of the period against the San Jose Sharks during the second period of Game 4 in the Western Conference Finals. RIC ERNST / PNG

that Malhotra has recovered to this stage, though the GM cautions any talk about a return, considering the seriousness of the eye injury. Vigneault decides to put Tambellini back in the lineup for the second game, replacing Oreskovich, because the coach wants more speed up front. The Sharks have hulking winger Ben Eager in the lineup as McLellan decides more physicality is necessary.

The Sharks take the lead for the second straight game when Couture scores on an early power play after a slashing penalty to Aaron Rome. The usually reliable Hansen is late on the backcheck and Couture scores on the rush. Vancouver pulls even when Daniel Sedin gets his seventh goal of the playoffs on a feed from brother Henrik during a power play. The Canucks take the lead thirty-nine seconds later when Torres converts a goalmouth pass from Ehrhoff after creating space in front by pushing Pavelski away from the net. San Jose makes it 2–2 later in the first period on another power-play marker by Marleau when Luongo can't smother a loose puck. A video review is needed and confirms the goal, with Daniel Sedin in the penalty box for cross-checking.

The second period sees the Canucks take the lead on a breakaway goal by defenceman Bieksa, who makes it look easy with a shot along the ice. Higgins makes the play possible, catching the Sharks unaware of his presence when he sits on the boards at the bench instead of jumping on the ice right away on a line change. Higgins jumps late and makes the pass that puts Bieksa into the clear. Later in the second, the hyper-aggressive Eager draws the ire of the Canucks and their fans when he runs Daniel Sedin into the boards from behind with a dangerous hit. Eager is penalized only two minutes, probably because Sedin got to his feet immediately, instead of taking a soccer-like rest on the ice to draw more attention.

In the third, the Canucks dominate as the home team strikes four times. Higgins scores on a pass into the slot by Mason Raymond after another penalty to Eager before Daniel Sedin gets his second of the game on yet another power play, this time with San Jose penalized for too many men on the ice. Rome scores another insurance goal after some effective cycling by the Sedins, and Raymond completes the Canucks scoring with their fourth power-play goal. All this happens before Eager scores late in the game, then stands over the Vancouver goaltender taunting Luongo. The late goal from Eager makes the final score 7–3. Vancouver leads the best-of-seven series 2–0 and keeps home ice advantage.

The Sharks are openly frustrated after losing their sixth straight Western Conference final game, having been swept in four by Chicago a year earlier. "You can't chase this team, they're too good," McLellan says of the Canucks. "You have to play with them or ahead of them." McLellan tries to mask the absurdity of Eager's play when the coach says, "I'll take Ben Eager's game without the penalties any night. An honest guy and he battled hard, but he can't march to the penalty box."

Bieksa draws the ire of the Sharks when he gets into a fight with the usually passive Marleau, but later it's determined that Marleau challenged Bieksa in an attempt to rally the San Jose troops. A rare playoff fight is one-sided in favour of the more experienced pugilist, Bieksa. "I thought he did a good job of sticking up for

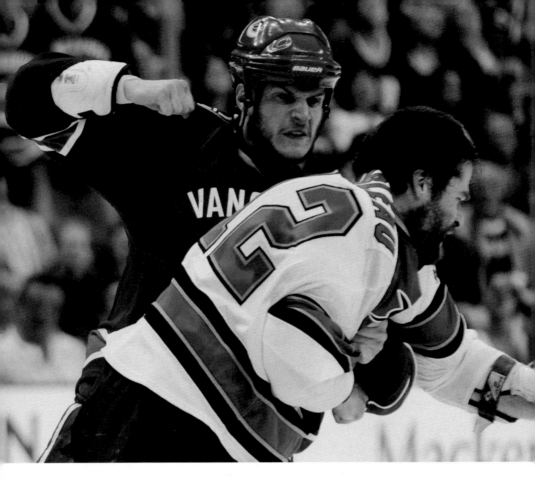

San Jose veteran Patrick Marleau bites off more than he can chew in a Game 2 tilt with rugged Canuck Kevin Bieksa. IAN LINDSAY/ PNG

himself and battling," Bieksa says of Marleau. "We came together and it just happened, a good battle." Marleau admits he asked for the bout. "It was a heat-of-the-moment kind of thing," he says. "It happens in hockey. I'm the one who dropped my gloves, so it was my decision, too." The Canucks win the game and the fight, but they aren't happy with the dangerous play of Eager, who insists he is just "finishing my checks." He's unapologetic for his actions.

Before the series moves to San Jose, the Canucks learn they've lost winger Mikael Samuelsson for the rest of the playoffs. He'll need surgery to repair a groin problem and an abductor tendon that hampered his skating and flared up again in the Nashville series. His veteran presence will be missed. It means more ice time for Higgins, who is skating on a sore foot, but has fit in nicely alongside Kesler. "He's playing with a lot of skill and determination," Vigneault says in praising Higgins. "He's doing a really good job for us."

The Canucks learn that Eager will not be suspended by the league for his dangerous hit from behind on Daniel Sedin. Vigneault doesn't agree with the NHL decision, saying in his mind Eager tried to injure a player who is potentially the most valuable in the league. Some of the obviously distraught Sharks get into some name-calling before Game 3 in San Jose. Clowe calls Lapierre a coward and Eager mouths off that Bieksa is a phony. The Canucks aren't taking the bait. "You've got to stay cool," Bieksa says. "If they are distracted with all the stuff going on, that's fine with us.

Vigneault opts to make two lineup alterations for the third game against the Sharks, inserting forwards Tanner Glass and Alex Bolduc to play on the fourth line in place of Tambellini and Cody Hodgson. The changes make little difference as the Canucks come out flat and quickly fall behind when Marleau scores early on the power play, converting a pass by Thornton following an elbowing penalty to Lapierre. The Sharks have fresh troops on their fourth line also, drawing inspiration from Jamie McGinn and Andrew Desjardins. Eager does not dress, however, as McLellan makes his point about un-disciplined play by sitting the veteran. Clowe on another power play and Marleau on a breakaway beat Luongo before the Canucks can get to the dressing room to re-group after being outshot 16–8 in the opening twenty minutes. San Jose leads 3–0 and the Shark Tank is going bananas over the sudden turn of events.

Vancouver continues to take unnecessary penalties in the scoreless second period. The Canucks twice have two-man advantages in the second, but can't convert as Salo is inaccurate with his shooting from the point. Burrows gives the Canucks some life early in the third with an unassisted goal from the slot, but the momentum doesn't last long as Boyle scores from the top of the circle when the Sharks hold a two-man advantage. The Canucks get close when Hamhuis and Bieksa score power-play goals later in the third, making the final margin 4–3 for San Jose. The Sharks are back in the series after a well-deserved victory. The defeat is even costlier as the Canucks lose defencemen Ehrhoff and Rome to injuries after they're hit hard by McGinn. The check on Ehrhoff looks legal, but the high hit on Rome is not and draws a major penalty.

The post-game analysis is simple: Vancouver gets into trouble early by taking penalties, an obvious sign that pre-game preparation was not what it's supposed to be. "When you give them those penalties and they score two, it hurts you," concedes Daniel Sedin. "They feel good about themselves and get confidence." The penalty-fest officiated by referees Brad Watson and Dan O'Rourke results in seventeen power plays, with San Jose getting the man advantage ten times. Kesler isn't happy with the Vancouver penalty killing. "Some games you don't deserve to win," he says. "This one, our [penalty kill] needs to be better."

Henrik Sedin talks about making adjustments, but finally concludes, "We need to be focused from the get-go." The Canucks have been in this position every series, winning early and then taking the foot off the pedal. "It's nothing new for us," Bieksa says, noting that the Vancouver defencemen are all comfortable playing with different partners when injuries occur. "Our depth is the strength of our team," Bieksa continues as he spins a positive outlook. "We said all year we had eight, nine quality defencemen. Now we get to show it."

The depth of the Vancouver defensive corps is going to be tested as Keith Ballard and Andrew Alberts will probably be needed in Game 4 after Rome suffers a head injury and Ehrhoff a shoulder problem. Vigneault also has another chip to play as rookie defencemen Chris Tanev, just twenty-one, arrives in San Jose between games, in case he's needed. Tanev is a first-year pro, but played with the poise of a veteran when pressed into duty twenty-nine times during the regular season.

Canucks head coach Alain Vigneault talks to the media prior to Game 3 of the Western Conference Finals. RIC ERNST/PNG

To a man, the Canucks vow they must stop the parade to the penalty box. In the first three games, Vancouver outscored San Jose 8–3 when the teams were at even strength. "Five-on-five, we're the better team," says Kesler. "I need to be better and we need to be better as a team, and we're going to be." Kesler plays about twenty-three minutes a game on average, the most of any Vancouver forward, and has his work cut out keeping track of Thornton and/or Marleau. Vigneault believes Kesler is an elite athlete who can handle the workload. "He's working real hard," says the Canuck coach. "I'm confident that things are going to work out."

In the San Jose dressing room, team captain Thornton concedes the Canucks still control the series, but figures the Sharks can pull even if they get the lead early in the game, just like in Game 3. "We've got to come out with desperation and get the first goal and get on them as quick as we can," he says.

Vigneault makes his adjustments defensively for Game 4. He keeps Hamhuis with Bieksa because it's his best pairing. Vigneault moves Edler alongside Salo and then surprises everyone when he inserts the rookie Tanev to play with Ballard in the third pairing. It's a risky move as this is Tanev's first NHL playoff game. A year ago Tanev was just finishing his freshman year at the Rochester Institute of Technology. Now he's in the cauldron of the Shark Tank.

The first period of Game 4 sees the Canucks take four consecutive penalties. Luongo makes ten saves as the penalty-kill unit holds off the Sharks. Vancouver gets another penalty before the tide turns in the second period. It begins with Ballard delivering a well-timed hip check that sends McGinn tumbling head over heels to the ice. Ballard is in position to make the spectacular play because of the perfect positioning of partner Tanev. Ballard has wanted an opportunity to show what he can do. The Canucks take notice and suddenly there's a swing in momentum.

Referees Kelly Sutherland and Eric Furlatt play a role in the change of the flow of the game as they assess San Jose four straight penalties. The Canucks strike quickly, scoring three times while on five-on-three power plays. The three goals come in a span of one minute and fifty-five seconds, all after faceoff wins in the San Jose zone, two by Henrik Sedin and another by Kesler. Kesler scores the first power-play goal from the left circle, one-timing an accurate shot on a pass from Salo. Niemi has no chance to make the save. Salo scores the next two goals with shots from the high slot, both on passes from Henrik Sedin.

The Canucks have applied an entirely new look on the five-on-three setup. Kesler has moved to the left circle instead of being in front of the net. That job goes to Burrows as he moves into traffic in front of the goalkeeper. Kesler, Salo and Henrik form a triangle or umbrella formation, with Daniel Sedin moving into the mid-slot or just off the net depending on where he's needed in order to assure possession for Vancouver. The five-man unit has never looked better. What's even more remarkable about the three, quick-strike Vancouver goals is that they are scored ten, nine and fifteen seconds after faceoff wins.

The Canucks get another goal, this one from Burrows on a two-on-one rush, early in the third period and lead

by four, with Henrik Sedin assisting on every goal. San Jose gets late goals, from Desjardins and Clowe, but loses Thornton late in the game when he's checked hard by Torres. Then, just as the game ends, Clowe punches Kesler in the face. The Canucks have gotten under the thin skins of the Sharks and won 4–3 to take a 3–1 series lead back to Vancouver, where they can wrap things up at Rogers Arena and advance to the Stanley Cup final for the first time since 1994.

"We know we're close," says Luongo, trying to control his enthusiasm between games. "We know we're right there, one step away. It's so much fun to come to the rink every day." Vigneault realizes imaginations can wander in these situations and stresses his team needs to be focused and bring the right intensity and emotion to the fifth game in the series. "That's where I believe our leadership group is going to come in and make sure everybody understands what needs to be done," says the coach.

Tanev, the cool-as-a-cucumber rookie, has experienced his post-season baptism in two pro leagues, having played in the American Hockey League playoffs with the Manitoba Moose for seven games before being recalled by the Canucks. He's not your typical wide-eyed, star-gazing newcomer. He's intently focused on a chance of a lifetime. "Just looking forward to being around the guys for a couple more weeks," says the Toronto-raised defenceman.

The Canucks are rolling again

Vancouver Canucks Alex Burrows, Chris Tanev and Dan Hamhuis, front to back, line up with San Jose Sharks Logan Couture, Patrick Marleau and captain Joe Thornton, front to back, during the third period of Game 4 in San Jose.

RIC ERNST/PNG

as they have their special teams back in order, scoring on three of five power plays and killing off five short-handed situations. The coaching staff has made adjustments, the Sedins have their touch back, Salo is hitting the net with his shots and Luongo is strong in goal, turning aside thirty-three of thirty-five shots. Life is good again for the Canucks after hitting a bump on the long playoff road. Taking a punch in the mouth is well worth it when the season-long objective comes more clearly into sight.

Game 5 and Rogers Arena is rocking, starting in warm-up as both teams have altered lineups. Vigneault moves Victor Oreskovich onto the fourth line in place of Bolduc in hopes of getting a harder forecheck. Oreskovich is a bigger body and shows more of a willingness to make contact. The Sharks decide to give Pavelski a bigger role and put the slick centre on a line with Clowe and Setoguchi. Couture, the rookie, is moved to right wing with Thornton and Marleau. Gone from the top six is Heatley, who appears to have a hand injury that hampers his shooting.

The Canucks respond to the urging of their fans by scoring in the first period when Burrows converts a pass from Henrik Sedin after the Vancouver captain gains possession on a turnover in the Sharks zone. The Vancouver penalty killing is reliable again as the Canucks kill off a two-man disadvantage in the first, after calls on Henrik Sedin for hooking and Kesler for slashing. The Canucks are two short for a minute and twenty-four seconds. Less than a minute after they're back at full strength, Vigneault calls a time out because his defence is bagged, dead tired from strenuous penalty killing. A lot of energy is expended when shorthanded. Six seconds after the team time out, there's a television time out that also helps players in their recovery. San Jose fires fifteen shots at Luongo in the first without scoring.

Vigneault tries to use four lines in the second period so that some of his overtaxed players like Kesler get more rest between shifts. The rookie Hodgson makes a key contribution when he wins a defensive-zone faceoff. Kesler gives the Canucks and fans a huge scare in the second period when he's helped to the bench with some sort of lower body injury. He appears to injure a hip or groin when he tries to chase down Boyle while killing a penalty. There's no contact on the play, but Kesler is in terrible pain. He goes to the dressing room and just seconds later Marleau ties the score when he tips a long point shot by Boyle, the puck deflecting past Luongo off the glove of defender Ballard. It's a fluke goal, but a reward for the Sharks as Boyle smartly directs his shot at the net instead of making a pass. There's a sigh of relief in the arena when Kesler returns to the Vancouver bench late in the second. He's skating rather gingerly when he takes a shift with his line, definitely not having the powerful stride that's a trademark of his game.

San Jose has a 25–12 advantage in shots on goal after forty minutes and keeps pushing in the third when Setoguchi scores twenty-four seconds into the period after a mistake by Luongo. The Vancouver goalie comes charging out of the net in an attempt to clear a loose puck—and loses the race, with a defender falling and leaving Setoguchi with an open net to give the Sharks the 2–1 lead. Kesler continues to struggle in the third, but his

Canucks defenceman Kevin Bieksa scored two big goals on San Jose Sharks goalie Antti Niemi in Western Conference Finals, the second one counting for an overtime win.

IAN LINDSAY/PNG

coach understands the competitive nature of his best two-way player. When the Canucks pull Luongo for an extra attacker in the last minute, Kesler is on the ice. Vigneault's faith in Kesler is rewarded when Kesler deflects in a shot by Henrik Sedin with 13.2 seconds left in regulation time, and the Canucks head into overtime with their objective still in reach.

In the first overtime period, Luongo makes another sixteen saves, often flashing his catching glove to make sensational stops, his best on a high wrist shot by Kyle Wellwood and on a Ryane Clowe redirection. He's on top of his game, much like he was in Game 7 of the deciding overtime game against Chicago in the first round. The second overtime session lasts just over ten minutes before a sudden conclusion in the San Jose zone would trigger the release of green and blue confetti and near bedlam at the Rog.

The Canucks have won 3–2 on a bizarre bounce at 10:18. Edler's high dump-in along the boards on the right side caroms off a metal stanchion on the glass and bounces to Bieksa in the middle of the ice near the blue line. Most of the players on both teams don't see the bouncing puck, thinking it has gone into the stands. It hasn't, and Bieksa quickly fires a floating shot that fortuitously bounces twice before eluding the surprised Niemi, ending the series and sending the Canucks to the NHL championship final.

Fans start yelling, "We want the Cup! We want the Cup!" Bieksa and teammates engage in a wild celebration and some of the Canucks nearly fall as the confetti makes footing treacherous. Burrows picks up the puck and guards the souvenir. "I just tried to put it on the net," Bieksa explains later. "When it went in, I just yelled out, 'Let's go to the Cup.' It's an ugly goal, but one we'll definitely take."

The Canucks are Western Conference champions for a third time, despite being outshot 54–34 in Game 5. NHL deputy commissioner Bill Daley brings out the Clarence

OVERLEAF: Vigneault hugs assistant coach Newell Brown as Canucks pour off the bench to celebrate Kevin Bieksa's conference winner against the Sharks. RIC ERNST/PNG

Campbell Trophy for presentation and Canucks captain Henrik Sedin poses with Daley and the trophy, but never touches the hardware as it is considered bad luck. The Canucks are after a much more significant trophy.

The windup of the San Jose series sees the Canucks get terrific goaltending from Luongo, a goal from the resilient Kesler and a huge break on Bieksa's shot, which he nearly missed when it bounced again just as he connected. "The only guy that knew where the puck was... was Kevin Bieksa," says McLellan in his post-game comments. "He actually bounced it into the net. It's one of those things that you absolutely have no control over. When you watch the replay, the officials didn't know where it was, Nemo didn't know where it was. Nothing we can do about it."

Vigneault praises his players for their efforts, most notably Kesler and Luongo. The coach calls Luongo "phenomenal" and Kesler "game." Luongo has stopped eighty-seven shots in the last two games against the Sharks. Vigneault is nearly at a loss for words, he's so delighted. Kesler tries to put things in perspective regarding Luongo and his ability to perform in big games when he offers, "He beat me at the Olympics, so there goes that theory out the window." Yes, Luongo has come up huge in ending series in overtimes against Chicago and San Jose, plus winning the Olympics in overtime.

"Just like his old Florida days," Burrows says about Luongo facing so many shots. "He looked big and played with confidence." The Sedins and Burrows help wear down the San Jose defence with their skating and puck possession in the final game, plus they forecheck with renewed purpose. "This is right up there with an

Olympic gold for us," says Henrik. "An Olympic gold medal is great, but it's a tournament where you get a few bounces and you're there. This is way tougher."

It takes the Canucks eighteen games to reach the Stanley Cup final for the first time in seventeen years. They have injuries, but will have some time off to rest for a final series only a few get to participate in during their careers. "I feel great," says the banged-up Kesler. "We're going to the Stanley Cup final and we finished off a pretty good team." Twelve playoff wins. Just four to go.

OVERLEAF: In a display of high spirits reminiscent of the 2010 Olympics, Vancouver fans packed the downtown to cheer their team on big-screen TVs. JASON PAYNE/PNG

## CHAPTER SIX

"I think it was good to feel that Chara's not a monster. I mean, he's good, but you can work him, you can make plays against him."
—Henrik Sedin reflects on playing
against Zdeno Chara

Better late than never

The Canucks have a long rest before they meet the Boston Bruins in the Stanley Cup final. Vancouver players get eight days between games while the Bruins go the limit with seven games against the Tampa Bay Lightning in the Eastern Conference final, finally prevailing 1–0 behind the shutout netminding of Tim Thomas and a goal by Nathan Horton. Boston gets a five-day break between series.

Meanwhile, Canucks two-way star Ryan Kesler needs time off so his mid-to-lower body injury can be treated. There are lots of other bumps and bruises to be iced and massaged, but Kesler is the one who gets most of the attention from trainer Mike Burnstein. Kesler tries to make light of the situation, saying he went to the dressing room last game because "I just had to call my wife. I thought I left the iron on." But there are doubts

144

about how healthy Kesler will be for the opener of the final series of the year against a team that plays a tight, physical game.

"I think we're prepared physically to go through it," Vancouver centre Henrik Sedin offers before adding, "and mentally it's good to get recharged and re-energized. I don't think it would matter if we had two, three or five days." The Sedin twins have played ten NHL seasons with the Canucks and figure they are almost Vancouverites. "We pretty much grew up here," says Henrik. "We were twenty when we came over [from Sweden]. You look at pictures from back then, we were different guys. So it's been a long journey and it's very special. Ninety percent of our time we spend here. We have friends here, we had our kids here. They're Canadians." It's like the Canucks have two captains because Henrik and Daniel are so alike.

Reaching the Cup final is special for each Vancouver player for varying reasons. For defenceman Sami Salo,

Nobody was immune to Canuck fever. WARD PERRIN/PNG

145

whose career is in the homestretch, it means he can share the experience with his kids. Salo's only regret is that his father passed away in 1995, before the Finlander played his first NHL game with the Ottawa Senators.

The Canucks have drawn a difficult assignment against the Bruins, a team that edged the Canucks 3–1 in league play back in late February when Vancouver product Milan Lucic was in on every Boston goal. There is a belief in the Canuck dressing room that Boston performs a lot like Nashville because the Bruins have size on defence and play with great physicality. "They have some

Mark Recchi takes a shot on goalie Luongo during Game 1 of the finals. The NHL's oldest active player at 43, Recchi had a strong series. RIC ERNST/PNG

big bodies that can bang us around," Luongo notes. "We've seen pretty much every type of style. I think what matters most is the way we play and execute our game plan."

In the days leading up to the opener, there's increasing speculation Malhotra will return to the lineup much earlier than anticipated. He's practising with the team and, to a man, players cite the leadership Malhotra brings to the Canucks. "He brought a lot of accountability to our locker room," Alex Burrows says. "He is the first one to stand up and admit when he's not playing well. He will tell you that and he'll make it black and white. That really helps us out." Malhotra wears a full face shield in practice, eleven weeks after his injury. He takes time to thank everyone who helped him after his eye injury, including former Canucks defenceman Mattias Ohlund, who suffered a similar injury that nearly derailed his career.

Vigneault and his staff have plenty of time to plan for Game 1 against Boston. They must decide what line will go against the Bruins, top unit of David Krejci with wingers Lucic and Horton. It's a no-brainer that Bieksa and Hamhuis will be the defensive pairing against Krejci and Co. Just how the Canucks attack Thomas and the Boston defence is another matter of concern. The Canucks need to find a way to penetrate the top Boston defensive pairing of Zdeno Chara and Dennis Seidenberg. Chara is a monster at 6-foot-9, while Seidenberg has surprised in the playoffs with his ability to play big minutes effectively. Vigneault will be matching strategy against Boston coach Claude Julien, once his teammate in the minors with the Salt Lake City Golden Eagles in the Central

Hockey League. There are subplots galore as game time approaches.

Game 1 at Rogers Arena has many wacky developments. The Bruins use the towering Chara in front of the Vancouver net on the Boston power play, trying to distract Luongo. The strategy doesn't work. There are plenty of scrums after the whistle, a definite Boston ploy. Burrows gets a mouth full of glove from Boston's Patrice Bergeron and apparently takes a bite to taste the leather. No extra penalty is assessed, much to the dismay of the Bruins. The Canucks suffer a deflating injury in the second period when Hamhuis lands awkwardly after hip-checking Lucic. Hamhuis doesn't return and the Canucks rotate five defencemen the rest of the way.

Luongo and Thomas are at the top of their games. Luongo faces thirty-six shots and Thomas thirty-four. It looks like overtime looms—until the final minute of regulation. The game comes to a sudden end when Torres scores an unexpected goal with 18.5 seconds left in the third, converting a cross-ice pass from Jannik Hansen after Kesler pounces on a turnover near the Boston blue line. Final score: 1–0 Vancouver. Chara was on the ice on his knees for the only goal against. The Bruins leave the ice stunned. What just hit them?

"It's pretty simple hockey," Torres says later. "Get pucks deep and try to work their defence. "Kes made a heads-up play holding onto the puck and got it to Hansen. I just tried to get open." Hansen says he could hear Torres yelling for the pass above the uproar of the hometown crowd. It was a fitting end because the unit of Torres, Hansen and Lapierre combined for ten shots on goal, not bad for a supposed checking unit.

Vigneault had Kesler on the ice in the last minute, instead of Lapierre, just in case there was a faceoff in the Boston zone.

Raffi Torres scores the game winner on Bruins goalie Tim Thomas with 18.5 seconds left in Game 1.

RIC ERNST/PNG

Even though Malhotra doesn't make his much-anticipated return to the lineup, he still influences the outcome. Torres praises Malhotra for taking the time to preach a positive approach that Torres gratefully adopts. "He just said go out there and relax, and at the end of the day, your game is meat and potatoes, and don't try to do anything outside your element," Torres recalls.

"He puts that in my head every day and I talk to him after every period. A couple of words of wisdom from a guy who knows what he's talking about."

The Canucks play a three-line game for most of the opener as Vigneault elects to go with players he trusts the most. Torres plays twelve minutes and fifty-two seconds, Hansen 15:26 and Lapierre 13:03. Hansen gets more ice time because he kills penalties on a regular basis. Kesler plays an amazing 24:23, considering he's still labouring with his injury.

But there's a huge problem on the horizon for the Canucks. They could be without defender Hamhuis for the rest of the series. He plays only eleven shifts and 8:09 in the Cup opener. Team officials list Hamhuis as day-to-day, which usually means he's not playing any-time soon. Vigneault has a tough decision to make be-fore Game 2. Does he replace Hamhuis with Ballard, or Andrew Alberts, or rookie Chris Tanev? Once again the Vancouver depth will be tested.

On the bright side, Luongo is at the top of his game. "When he gets hot, he is the best goalie in the world," boasts Daniel Sedin. "Hopefully he will keep it going." Speaking of getting going, the Sedins need to have more of a presence in the offensive zone, where they have Chara and Seidenberg as constant companions. Daniel does manage eight shots on goal, but can't beat Thomas. Henrik has no shots on goal, but still feels comfortable with his game.

"I think we played a real good road game, to be honest with you," Julien says during his post-game re-marks. "But, obviously, in the third they were the better team. It got away from us." As for Vigneault, he looks at the combined seventy shots on goal. "Well, we've got two of the best goaltenders in the league battling it out," he analyzes. "So obviously scoring is going to be a challenge for both teams."

The unlikely hero of the night is Torres, the hard-hitting redhead who goes to the greasy areas near the goalmouth. Here's a guy who spent most of the past summer waiting near the phone as an unrestricted free agent. The call finally came August 25, 2010, from Gillis. The player who grew up in Toronto idolizing Wendel Clark of the Maple Leafs now has dedicated followers of his own in Vancouver.

Dancing the bhangra to the Dhol drums, thousands of fans celebrate Game 1 win at "Canucks Corner" at Scott Road and 72nd Avenue in Surrey. LES BAZSO/PNG

## CHAPTER SEVEN

*"It won't be easy. Until you win a road game,
you aren't in control of any series."*
—An overview by Alex Burrows
on the final series

Wrapping it up in eleven seconds

There are two days between games early in the final and plenty of time to debate issues arising from the opener. The Bruins want the league to suspend Burrows for his impromptu chomp on the gloved hand of Bruins centre Patrice Bergeron. Burrows pleads innocent, suggesting it was Bergeron who stuck his glove in Burrows' face during a getting-to-know-you scrum. NHL senior vice-president of hockey operations Mike Murphy consults many of his cohorts before ruling there will be no suspension. Murphy is the league's disciplinarian in the Cup final when Colin Campbell, senior NHL vice-president of hockey operations, abandons those duties because his son, Gregory, plays for the Bruins. Murphy issues a statement reading, "After reviewing the incident, including speaking with the on-ice officials, I can find no conclusive evidence that Alex Burrows intentionally bit the finger of Patrice Bergeron."

Video evidence seems to suggest otherwise, but at the time of the incident referees Stephen Walkom and Dan O'Rourke assessed Bergeron and Burrows with roughing minors. Claude Julien accepts the decision and says his team is moving on. "We're not the type of team that whines and cries about these things," the Boston bench boss insists. Bergeron also downplays the finger faux pas. "I mean, we were both face-washing each other," he says. "I didn't mean to put my finger in his mouth. Why would I do that?"

The NHL has handed down suspensions before for finger biting indiscretions, but not this time, which sits just fine with a relieved Canucks coach Alain Vigneault, who doesn't need to lose his top right winger. "To tell you

Digital controversy erupts after Boston centre Patrice Bergeron claims he was bitten on the finger during scrum with Alex Burrows. Burrows responds with 2 goals and an assist. IAN LINDSAY/PNG STAFF PHOTO

the truth, I didn't pay a lot of attention," Vigneault says when asked if he spoke with league officials. "Nobody talked to me, from management or the league, so I've been focused on getting ready [for Game 2]." There's no formal hearing for Burrows, who is smart enough to keep his fingers off the hot-button issue between games. He understands, after tasting leather, the Bruins definitely will have him on their radar the rest of the series.

Vigneault has his work cut out because he must adjust his defence following the injury to Hamhuis, whose steadiness will be missed. Keith Ballard seems like the likely choice. He patiently waits on the sideline, hoping he gets to play in his first Cup final game. "I think all the guys who have not been playing have been approaching it exactly the same way," says the diplomatic Ballard. "We are working real hard. We are pulling for the same thing. We all want to win the Cup. We want to get our name on it." Ballard has experience against Eastern Conference teams after playing two years with the Florida Panthers. So does Andrew Alberts, who has played for Boston, Philadelphia and Carolina. Alberts, in fact, broke into the NHL in 2005 with the Bruins. Ballard was teammates in Florida with present Boston players Gregory Campbell, Nathan Horton and Dennis Seidenberg.

Vigneault isn't tipping his hand about his Game 2 strategy, even when asked if Malhotra will make his long-anticipated return. Malhotra is still listed as day-to-day. Malhotra practises with the Canucks at the University of BC between games and tells reporters he understands the severity of his eye injury. His right eye still looks puffy after a secret procedure on the eve of the Cup final. "I realize the intensity of the moment and realize the intensity of play has picked up since I last played [March 16]," Malhotra says. "This is not me wanting to have a sentimental shift out there and be part of it all. It's the fact I feel I could contribute something to the team." Malhotra's continued presence around the team is viewed as a positive by Vancouver players, who earlier listened to him sombrely tell them they'd have to win the Stanley Cup without him. Players admit they

Manny Malhotra's remarkable comeback from a potentially career-ending eye injury gave team morale a big boost going into Game 2.

RIC ERNST/PNG

can't imagine what Malhotra has gone through, especially the doubt over his future.

For a team with a 1–0 lead in the final, the Canucks have a lot of question marks going into the second game at home. Vancouver fans begin their chant "Manny, Manny" during warm-up when Malhotra takes the pre-game skate. Vigneault makes his final lineup decision just minutes before game time, inserting Malhotra and Alberts in place of Bolduc and Hamhuis. Bolduc has been used sparingly, appearing in three playoff games and averaging less than four minutes. On the other hand, Hamhuis averages twenty-four minutes and fifty seconds because he usually plays in the top defensive pairing.

Rock 'n' roll legend Randy Bachman stirs up the crowd even more when he joins house band the Odds for a lively rendition of "Takin' Care of Business" just before the opening faceoff. It gets even louder when Malhotra takes his first shift in nearly three months just two minutes and fifty seconds into the game. Malhotra hasn't lost his touch in the faceoff circle, winning his first draw from Boston's Chris Kelly.

The Canucks have their tactics in order against the Bruins' top line, using Kesler, Raymond and Higgins to check the David Krejci unit, with Bieksa and Rome on defence. Vigneault switches things up occasionally, opting for the Sedin line against Krejci to keep Boston guessing. Kesler is on the receiving end of a heavy check from Bruins defenceman Johnny Boychuk early in the game. The Canucks respond when fourth-liner Oreskovich throws three bone-rattling checks on one shift. Both teams are forechecking furiously. Luongo has his mask knocked off when he stops a high shot from Michael Ryder to thwart a two-on-one rush by the Bruins.

Moments later, the Canucks take the lead when Burrows scores on a power play with Boston captain Zdeno Chara in the penalty box for interference after bulldozing Kesler to the ice. The shot by Burrows on a pass from Higgins barely dribbles into the net off the arm pad of Bruins goalie Tim Thomas. Vancouver's second unit on the power play is successful after the first unit is denied. Malhotra gets more work in the second period, five shifts in all covering two minutes and fifty-two seconds. He's used to kill penalties, mostly with forward partner Maxim Lapierre. Luongo faces fourteen shots in the second and makes a huge stop on Krejci before the Bruins finally flex their offensive muscle.

Boston surges into a 2–1 lead when Milan Lucic and Mark Recchi score in a span of two minutes and thirty-five seconds. Lucic deposits a rebound after Luongo stops a point shot by Boychuk. Recchi, the oldest player in the series at forty-three, scores on a power play by tipping a shot launched by Chara. The Canucks push back later in the second and Jannik Hansen is denied by Thomas after a slick setup from Kesler, leaving Hansen shaking his head. Meanwhile, Rome on the Vancouver defence is having trouble coping with the speed of the Boston forwards.

Even though Burrows has his emotions under control, one of the Canucks doesn't. Lapierre, the one-time Montreal Canadiens agitator, decides he wants to stir things up. Lapierre pokes his gloved fingers into the face of Patrice Bergeron, attempting to draw a response, perhaps even a penalty. With the Bruins leading, Bergeron doesn't go for the bait in a reverse re-enactment of the Burrows affair. After the game, Lapierre notes, "I was raised to hate the Bruins. That's the way it is for pretty much everybody in Montreal."

In the third period, the Sedin twins begin to assert themselves for the Canucks, but can't solve the unpredictability of Thomas, who flips, flops and seemingly flies through the goal area when necessary. The Vancouver power play is ineffective against Boston's diligent penalty-kill unit, which forces the Canucks to the outside, closer to the sideboards than the net. The Bruins have a definite plan and execute the strategy efficiently. Or is it just that Chara and Seidenberg own the space around the Boston net because they're so physical?

Finally, midway through the third, the Canucks find a way to beat Thomas. Daniel Sedin pulls the trigger from the left circle on a setup from Burrows and beats the Boston netminder up high while Thomas is down. Tie game, 2–2. Burrows seems to be everywhere for the Canucks. He's not munching on fingers this game. He's driving the Bruins crazy with his inspiring persistence in the Boston zone.

In overtime, Vigneault smartly starts Burrows and the Sedins. What a marvellous decision by the Canucks coach, who could have opened with his checkers. It takes just eleven seconds for the Canucks and Burrows to give Vancouver a 3–2 victory. Burrows scores his second goal of the game and third point of the night when he works his way around the slower Chara and the Boston net before depositing a wraparound shot into an open goalmouth. Thomas is late moving post-to-post, having overcommitted to the right side on the initial rush.

Wrapping it up in eleven seconds

Bedlam erupts once again at Rogers Arena. Randy Bachman and the Odds quickly break out "Takin' Care of Business," after Burrows leaps into the air in celebration. Burrows throws in a somersault for good measure, then his bow-and-arrow routine to honour the late Luc

Henrik Sedin celebrates Canucks' second goal in Game 2, scored by brother Daniel on a setup from Alex Burrows. MARK VAN MANEN/PNG

Bourdon, a good friend and teammate from years past. Burrows draws the spotlight as the overtime hero for the second time in the playoffs. He scored in sudden-death to eliminate Chicago and now he's given the Canucks a 2–0 series lead in the Stanley Cup final.

"He was so calm under pressure," Kesler says. "He just has a knack. Some players have it and he's got a knack for big goals." Burrows, thirty, has learned the hard way after going undrafted by NHL teams

Fans go wild in downtown Vancouver as outdoor TV screens show Alex Burrows scoring overtime winner in Game 2.

JASON PAYNE/PNG

and working his way up through the hardscrabble East Coast Hockey League and the American Hockey League. He once was best known for his agitating ways and ability to kill penalties. Now the survivor from Pincourt, Quebec, is an offensive force.

"The first few years of my career I was on the bench for those kinds of moments," says Burrows. "You have to pay your dues. I think I've worked hard to be there." Burrows took time to acknowledge a telephone conversation he had with his father Rodney in Montreal, after the opening game of the final when the topic mostly was his finger-biting episode with Bergeron. "I hurt my dad's feelings a little bit, and maybe my mom's," admits Burrows. "My dad said, 'Go out there and score some goals. That's what's really going to piss them off even more.' I listened to his advice."

Following Game 2, Julien again insists the Bruins are a better team than they've shown. "We didn't come here just to roll over," he says. Vigneault is comfortable with the results, noting the Canucks have been strong in their third periods all season. "We can push the pace and create scoring chances," he says. "I thought we did. I thought that line [the Sedins with Burrows] really took over in the third and spent a lot of time in their end, wearing down their defence. It paid off for us."

So did the inclusion of Malhotra, with the "Manny" chants an inspiration for all. Malhotra says he was nervous, but settled down to play thirteen shifts, good for seven minutes and twenty-six seconds. He won six of seven faceoffs. "I'll become more confident with the puck again, try to make more plays, skate with the puck," Malhotra predicts. "I think playing seven

161

minutes in my first game back is a good transition into things."

"What a boost," says Jeff Tambellini, who plays on the fourth line with Malhotra and Oreskovich. "The guy steps in and doesn't miss a beat." The Bruins beat a retreat to Boston while the Canucks bask in their good fortunes after two home games.

CHAPTER EIGHT

"Luckily, it's not aggregate score. It's not Champions League. It's the Stanley Cup final."
—Kevin Bieksa puts his spin on the series

Rome is Beantown's public enemy No. 1

Boston is down two games in the Stanley Cup final, but one thing the Bruins have established is they will play a physical brand of hockey, forechecking hard in the Vancouver zone and making life miserable for the Canucks in the Boston end. The Bruins have put the lumber on the Canucks after almost every whistle, with penalties rarely called as game officials look the other way. It's apparent the referees don't want to make many decisions that give either team an advantage. It's a difficult situation for the Canucks, who had the league's best power play during the regular season. Vancouver doesn't have an enforcer as such, relying instead on the threat of the power play to discourage the opposition from taking liberties.

The Bruins have a mindset that encourages physical play at nearly every opportunity. It's a team thing, with

Thousands of Canucks fans lined Georgia Street and Hamilton to watch every move of Game 3 of the Stanley Cup playoffs on a giant screen. MARK VAN MANEN/PNG

everyone chipping in. Vigneault doesn't seem overly concerned before Game 3 in Boston. "I think if you look at the stat sheet, at the end of the day we're hitting as hard as they are," Vigneault says, adding that Bieksa went down briefly with an injury the previous game when slashed in the back of the leg by Boston forward Rich Peverley. "Kevin didn't get hit by [a bodycheck]. He got a cheap shot on the back of the knee."

Vigneault expresses confidence in defenceman Andrew Alberts after the Boston College grad led the Canucks with six hits in the second game, playing just over twelve minutes while helping replace the injured Hamhuis. Alberts isn't the most mobile defender, but he's willing to put his body on the line after recovering from an injury suffered the previous series. Alberts was thought to be expendable before the season as the Canucks stockpiled defencemen by adding Hamhuis through free agency and trading for Ballard. Alberts came to training camp a little lighter than the previous season and the improved quickness made him a better defender, allowing the Canucks to trade holdover Shane O'Brien just before opening night. "He was pretty intense and that's what we expected," Vigneault says in describing Alberts when his defensive partner was Ehrhoff in Game 2. "He played well—physical and was a high percentage with the puck."

Luongo looks forward to playing in Boston because that's where he played his first NHL game in the 1999–2000 season when he was a rookie with the New York Islanders. He got his first NHL win against the Bruins and also his first shutout in an NHL game. "It's a pretty good history, I'd say," Luongo beams. In his last fourteen playoff games, starting with the 2–1 overtime decision over Chicago in Game 7 of that series, Luongo has allowed only twenty-seven goals.

Boston coach Claude Julien has one lineup change in mind for Game 3. He inserts rugged winger Shawn Thornton into the fourth line to step up the hitting and forechecking. Thornton was mainly a fighter earlier in his career before learning to contribute as a checker and occasional goal scorer. The Bruins pull out all stops before the game by having popular Hockey Hall of Fame member Cam Neely mingle with fans before the game, which marks the twenty-sixth anniversary of his trade to Boston by the Canucks, the team that drafted him.

Manny Malhotra takes the opening faceoff for the Canucks after being cleared by doctors to continue his inspiring comeback after eye surgery. Back in Vancouver, a crowd of more than 14,000 gathers in Rogers Arena to watch the away game on the replay screen and cheers enthusiastically when Malhotra gets the early nod from Vigneault. Vancouver carries the game during the nervously played first five minutes before the Bruins get a rude wakeup call. It comes in the form of a thunderous hit delivered by Canucks defenceman Aaron Rome on unsuspecting Nathan Horton. The Boston winger goes down hard, hitting the back of his head on the ice. He lies motionless and a hush comes over TD Garden.

Horton had just made a pass to a teammate near the boards and was looking to his left, almost as if admiring his pass. He didn't see Rome coming. Rome made a split-second decision to deliver a check, with his shoulder glancing off the chest of Horton and up into the head area after the puck had gone a split-second earlier. Referees Stephen Walkom and Dan O'Rourke determined Rome would be assessed a major penalty and game misconduct. What many observers didn't know is that Thornton had chirped at Rome on the Vancouver bench not long before the hit on Horton. No one knows for sure what was said, but Rome delivered his huge hit shortly after a Thornton check on Vancouver's Alex Burrows. Horton is carried from the ice on a stretcher, his head immobilized. Rome has already disappeared down the tunnel on his way to the Vancouver dressing room.

The Canucks have Boston's attention now. The Bruins fire six shots at Luongo during the five-minute Rome penalty, but are unable to score. The first period remains scoreless when Bruins netminder Tim Thomas makes two saves on Mason Raymond following a turnover

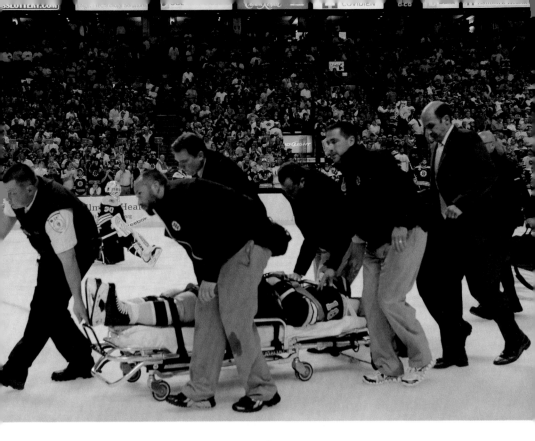

in the Boston zone. Peverley replaces Horton on Boston's top line with David Krejci and Milan Lucic to open the second period and it takes only eleven seconds for the Bruins to score, with a floater by Andrew Ference from the blue line deflecting behind the startled Luongo after Canucks defenceman Alex Edler broke his stick.

Bruins star winger Nathan Horton is wheeled out of TD Garden on a stretcher after a hard check by Canucks defenceman Aaron Rome in first period of Game 3. RIC ERNST/PNG/POSTMEDIA NEWS

The Canucks are back on their heels, unable to push forward. Mark Recchi scores for Boston on a power play when his pass deflects into the net off the stick of Vancouver's backchecking Ryan Kesler. Following a turnover by Daniel Sedin, the Bruins make it 3–0 when pesky Brad Marchand capitalizes after working his way around Kesler. Krejci scores the fourth Boston goal of the period on a rebound when the Canucks are caught flat-footed in the defensive zone. The wheels have fallen off. Now the Bruins push their physical game to another level, punishing the Canucks at every opportunity. Luongo doesn't want to come out of the game at 5–0 in the third period and Vigneault agrees to leave him in. Boston pumps fourteen shots at Luongo in the period and the final score ends 8–1 after Dan Paille shorthanded Recchi with his second of the game and Chris Kelly and Michael Ryder light up Luongo. The lone Vancouver goal comes from third-liner Jannik Hansen on a pass from Raffi Torres.

The Canucks are humbled and humiliated. They are pushed around, with captain Henrik Sedin uncere-moniously dumped by Boston goaltender Thomas with a rarely seen goaltender bodycheck in front of the net. Boston players are in full face-wash mode, using the tactic on nearly every stoppage. Walkom and O'Rourke hand out 145 minutes in penalties, but are unable to control the emotional rush the Bruins seem to enjoy, including bare-finger wagging at Burrows by Lucic and Recchi after whistles.

Vancouver has lost the third game for the third straight series, all on the road. The Canucks are weak on faceoffs and the once-vaunted power play is blanked in eight opportunities. They don't have enough resilience to save face. "Our power play, or lack of it, gave them mo-mentum," Vigneault says. "You know, that's been one of our biggest weapons all year long. It's kept the opposition real honest against us, especially on the road. Tonight, obviously, we weren't good enough. I'm confident that this group will be good enough come next game."

Luongo has been ventilated, thrown off his game by bizarre goals off deflections and even his own players. He tries to keep things in perspective. "At the end of the day, we have to realize we're up 2–1 and have a chance to win the next game and go home 3–1. That is what we're going to focus on the next twenty-four hours."

The Bruins are irate about the Rome hit on Horton that takes Boston's second-best post-season goal producer (eight) out of the series with a concussion. They believe it was a blindside hit, the kind the league wants to eliminate from the game. "It came from the blind side," insists Julien. "We'll let the league take care of it. They're trying to clean that out. Let's see where they go with that."

Naturally, Vigneault sees things differently than his coaching counterpart. "The hit was head-on, player

Dejected Canucks fan watches in horror as Boston scores 8 goals in a Game 3 blowout. MARK VAN MANEN/PNG

169

looking at his pass," Vigneault says in his post-game remarks. "It was a little bit late. I don't think that's the hit the league is trying to take out of the game. This is a physical game. You have big guys, fraction of a second to decide what's happening out there."

Vigneault isn't sure if the hit is a rallying point for the Bruins, but it sure seems that way. As for Rome, he says nothing after the game, wondering if he faces a suspension and, if so, for how long. Just the previous series he was injured when checked into the glass in San Jose. There was no suspension levied. "Romer is a real honest player," says Henrik Sedin as the captain defends his teammate. "I don't think it was blindside or anything like that. We came into a tough building, we killed a five-minute penalty off. But in the second period they get a break early and then it just snowballed from there." Did it ever! Now the resolve of the Canucks will be tested once again.

## CHAPTER NINE

"I don't think anyone can win if their top line isn't scoring."
    —Henrik Sedin states the obvious in Boston

Canucks firing blanks at Thomas

For the first time in the final, the Canucks have been outplayed by a wide margin. Tim Thomas has put the Bruins in position to stage a stirring comeback. Thomas stopped forty shots in the third game, compared with only thirty saves by Luongo as the Bruins crushed Vancouver 8–1. Doubt is creeping into Canucks Nation, but not Luongo. He remains optimistic the storm will pass. "This is the Stanley Cup final [and] I've waited my whole life to be here," Luongo says between games. "I'm not going to put my head down. But at the end of the day, I have to try to make more saves. I have to be better. This is part of goaltending. You have to have a short memory in this game."

So do many other Canucks after a beat-down in Boston. Alex Edler was minus-4 on defence for goals scored at even strength. Ryan Kesler and Christian Ehrhoff were minus-3. The only Vancouver player on the plus side of the ledger was steady defenceman Sami Salo at plus-1. The Canucks appeared distracted, perhaps by the one-sided score, but more likely by the growing aggressiveness of the Bruins. The Canucks haven't fared well in the many scrums after whistles.

In Boston, Vancouver players are quizzed about their dirty play, of all things. The Canucks are regarded as the hated aggressors after the Burrows bite in the first game and the Aaron Rome hit that concussed Nathan Horton. "Is that our image?" Henrik Sedin wonders.

Former Canuck Dave Babych attends the re-lighting of the Olympic Cauldron in Vancouver, hoping to fire up the home team. WAYNE LEIDENFROST/PNG

"Maybe in Boston, I don't know. I know what kind of group we have. We're a tight group and we're honest players. Maybe guys are going to cross the line a little bit, but I don't think we're the dirtiest team in the playoffs."

The Canucks are under tighter scrutiny than usual after the Rome incident. Kesler gets into a fight with Boston's Dennis Seidenberg midway through the final period of the second game, an element of the game that Kesler rarely participates in, especially this season when he's tried to turn the other cheek. "We have to realize our focus is to play hockey," insists Sedin. "That's something we've brought up already and we're going to give that a lot of attention." Vigneault readily agrees with his captain and prime team spokesman. "We've been a team that's been very disciplined all year, playing whistle to whistle," Vigneault states. "I think we might have got away from that a little. We're going to have to do a better job there."

They'll have to do it without Rome, who is slapped with a four-game suspension by NHL senior vice-president of hockey operations Mike Murphy, eliminating Rome from the rest of the Stanley Cup final. Murphy notes, "The hit by Rome was clearly beyond what is acceptable in terms of how late it was delivered after Horton had released the puck and it caused a significant injury."

Vigneault is furious with the interpretation of the hit and the decision to suspend. "In my opinion, that's not the right call," says Vigneault. "It was a little bit late, but anybody who has played this game knows you have to make a decision in a fraction of a second. He engaged in the hit. I don't know how the league can come up with that decision. It was a hockey play that went bad. He's not a dirty player and never has been and never will be. He's very emotional and very disappointed."

Rome issues a statement through the Canucks saying, "I want to express my concern for Nathan's well-being and wish him a quick and full recovery. I try to play this game with honesty and integrity. As someone who has experienced this type of injury, I am well aware of its serious nature and have no desire for another player to experience it." Bruins coach Claude Julien discloses that Horton is out of hospital the day after the incident and resting at home, probably facing a lengthy recovery. The Canucks now must determine a replacement for Rome. Keith Ballard is a possibility. So is rookie Chris Tanev. Ballard says his confidence is good despite a long layoff between assignments. He wants to show the coaching staff that he can be trusted in big games.

TD Garden is rocking again as the teams take the pre-game skate a half-hour before Game 4. The Bruins trot out the legendary Bobby Orr, probably the greatest defenceman of all-time, before the game to mingle with fans. He's wearing his retired No. 4 jersey. Orr waves a Boston flag with Horton's No. 18 on it. The Canucks have an unexpected supporter in the stands in Prime Minister Stephen Harper, who sings "O Canada" with other Canadians in the crowd along with long-time Boston anthem fist-pumper Rene Rancourt. Julien elects to use rookie forward Tyler Seguin to replace Horton in the lineup, with Rich Peverley remaining on the top line in Horton's spot, and Seguin slipping into the third unit with Chris Kelly and Michael Ryder. Vigneault inserts

Lonely but brave Bruins fans celebrate their team's Game 4 goal in a sea of Canucks fans on Georgia Street. STEVE BOSCH/PNG

Ballard and winger Tanner Glass in place of Rome and Tambellini.

The Canucks have a decent first period, outshooting Boston 12–6, but trail 1–0 when Peverley gets between defenders Edler and Salo to score. The Canucks are just 1-for-17 with the man advantage in the series after their power play fizzles late in the period. The Bruins again are mauling the Canucks, with Seidenberg laying on the lumber without worrying about being penalized for his leg chops by referees Dan O'Halloran and Kelly Sutherland. It seems like anything goes in this series as the Canucks start to slow down, especially Ballard on defence as he has trouble containing Boston's better forwards.

Boston scores twice in the second period in a span of two minutes and eighteen seconds to take command. Ryder fires home a harmless-looking wrist shot that flutters and beats Luongo on the glove side. Soft goal, for sure! Then it is Brad Marchand's turn as the Boston rookie winger converts a turnover near the net after appalling confusion on Ballard's part. In the final period, Peverley scores again and Schneider replaces Luongo for the rest of the game. Schneider stops all nine shots he faces. Luongo has allowed four goals on twenty shots. Game over, 4–0 Boston, but not before there's plenty of pushing and shoving, including Thomas and Seidenberg wrestling Alex Burrows to the ice in front of the Boston goal.

The Canucks seem to lack leadership. No one is stepping up to take charge, though Vancouver does outshoot the Bruins 38–29. Boston is 11–4 in the play-offs when the Bruins are outshot. Thomas ensures the shutout when he stops Chris Higgins on a third-period breakaway. The Bruins can take all the penalties they want because Vancouver is irrelevant on the power play. The Canucks misfired six times with the man advantage in Game 4. Now they've been outscored 12–1 in two games at Boston. "I did not play very well," admits Ballard, who is minus-2 for the night. "We didn't play well as a team and I didn't play well individually."

Two games ago, Luongo had looked forward to playing in Boston. After twelve goals against, Luongo appears to be in shock, something that Vigneault doesn't publicly agree with. "Lou's going to be fine," Vigneault says before the Canucks head back to Vancouver. "He's one of the best goaltenders in the league and we've got a lot of trust and faith in him and his ability to play well. He'll get himself ready to play Game 5."

Thomas has been the real gamer as the Bruins even the series at 2–2. He stops Ehrhoff seven times in the fourth game, although Ehrhoff's shot appears to lack any zip, perhaps because he still has a sore shoulder from the San Jose series. "He's taken a real bumpy road to get to the NHL," Julien says while praising Thomas, thirty-seven. "He's had so many obstacles in front of him that he's overcome, it makes him a battler. It makes him a perfect goaltender for our organization because that's what we are."

At this stage of the final, the Canucks could use some of Thomas's engagement in their game. The Sedins are taking a physical beating. They try to analyze the two losses with a soft explanation. "It's the playoffs, it doesn't matter what year it is, what team it is, you're not going to sweep someone in the finals," offers Henrik. "That's not going to happen. We won two at home. They

Canucks defenceman Keith Ballard drops to block a Michael Ryder shot in front of Luongo in Game 4. Ballard draws back into Canucks lineup to replace suspended Aaron Rome, but it isn't enough. RIC ERNST/PNG

won two here. Right now, Thomas is playing great and we're going to have to find a way to score."

Through four games, the Canucks have been out-scored 8–0 in second periods. They've taken their eye off the ball, suggests one analyst. Boston has its game nicely in place, namely chip, chase and check. "It's about execution and intensity," says Malhotra after his third game this post-season, adding Vancouver's overall game "has to be better."

CHAPTER TEN

"I've talked to him a lot about winning, about winning the Stanley Cup. He's a very emotional player and when he's emotionally involved and focused, he's a tremendous player."
—Chris Higgins about teammate Maxim Lapierre

Banking on the bounces

Canucks coach Alain Vigneault is under fire as the team returns home for Game 5 of the Stanley Cup final. Fans wonder why the team has scored only one goal in two games at Boston and why Luongo was not pulled earlier in both losses when it was obvious he was off his game. Vigneault has much to answer for, but he's careful to protect his players as they prepare for what many believe is the most important game Vancouver has played since Game 7 of the 1994 final. This time, importantly, it's the Canucks that have home ice advantage, something they competed for all season and attained by winning the Presidents' Trophy as the NHL's best team in the regular season.

"They're elite players and we've got to where we are today because our top players are on most nights," Vigneault says about Vancouver's best. "Obviously we need those guys to play up to their standards, and they will. We've faced adversity throughout the season in many shapes and forms. We're playing against a real strong opponent right now. But we're also a very good team. We've proved it in the past and we're going to set out to prove it [again]."

Many NHL insiders wonder if the Canucks are still drinking the Kool-Aid. Do the players still believe they're the better team? Have the Bruins got under the thin skin of the Canucks? Probably they have, if you read anything into an incident that happened late in the previous game when the Canucks got into a verbal spat with Boston's impish but effective winger Brad Marchand.

Excitement rises among the Canuck faithful as the Canucks return home for Game 5. JASON PAYNE/PNG

Marchand was assessed a rare triple-minor penalty, getting six minutes after high-sticking and manhandling Christian Ehrhoff, hitting Daniel Sedin well below the hips and dropping his gloves with Keith Ballard. Marchand also made a hand-washing gesture as he passed by the Vancouver bench at TD Garden in Boston. "That's something I shouldn't have done," Marchand says about the hand signal he gave the Canucks. "It was a little childish. They were yelling at me from the bench. That's just how I reacted. I wish I didn't do it."

The Canucks, on the other hand, should wish they weren't distracted so easily. Ryan Kesler and Alex Burrows are off their games. So are the Sedins. Luongo has been great at home, but abysmal away from Rogers Arena. The Canucks need to concentrate on the power play, which has produced just one goal in twenty-two advantages through four games. Vigneault tries to keep painting a positive picture for anyone who'll listen. "We're playing for the Stanley Cup final, two out of three in this great city and with these great fans," the coach says. "It doesn't get much better than this."

One Vancouver player enjoying the ride is Salo, who has a positive perspective because for many months he was unsure he'd be a participant. "It has been a great journey," Salo says, despite more than forty injuries, many of them so serious his career was in doubt. "If someone had said come June you'd be playing [in] the Stanley Cup finals, I think I would have laughed." In Salo's mind, the joke is on all the doubters over his ability to bounce back and be a reliable contributor on one of the best NHL teams. His wife, two daughters and a son are able to enjoy Sami's finest moment, something he's played for since growing up in faraway Turku, Finland.

Luongo also has waited years for this opportunity. "At the end of the day, we're two wins away from reaching the ultimate goal," he says. "I don't think it's time for us to be putting our heads down, or to not have any confidence." It's pretty simple what the Canucks must do against Boston. They need a return to form by Luongo, better execution on special teams, solidified defensive pairings and improved team discipline.

Like the Canucks, the Bruins also have a few skeletons in their playoff closet. Boston has a hideous 1–11 record in its three previous Stanley Cup final series, including four losses in five games against the Edmonton Oilers in 1990—the last time the Bruins reached the final when Mike Milbury was Bruins coach. It is Milbury, of all people, who on television during this series belittles the Sedins with a "Thelma and Louise" comparison. Yes, this is the same Milbury who once traded Luongo to the Florida Panthers when Milbury was general manager of the New York Islanders. Oh, and Milbury also dispatched now-Boston captain Zdeno Chara to the Ottawa Senators, with Alexei Yashin coming to the Isles.

So there is plenty to talk about before Game 5 and by opening faceoff, Vigneault has made another lineup change, this time opting to use rookie defenceman Chris Tanev in place of Ballard. Tanev has one game of NHL playoff experience, but at this stage he's clearly an upgrade on Ballard, who has fallen out of favour with the Vancouver coaching staff due to inconsistency.

Rogers Arena house band the Odds get the joint jumping with their rockin' audio and Luongo comes up

Roberto Luongo returns to Jennings Trophy form in Game 5 against the Bruins, staking his team to a 1–0 shutout. IAN LINDSAY/PNG

with an early save on Chris Kelly to deny a two-on-one Boston rush. The Canucks forecheck aggressively and the Bruins rely on their transition game to create scoring chances. Alex Edler is back in form as the Vancouver defenceman hands out jolting bodychecks. The Canucks are shorthanded three times in the first period, but the penalty-kill units are reliable, along with Luongo. They are denied a power play when referees Stephen Walkom and Dan O'Rourke elect to overlook what appears to be a spear after the whistle by Chara on Lapierre. The

Canucks' reputation for diving appears to be costing the team once again. Late in the opening period, Burrows is called for embellishment after he's pitchforked to the ice by hulking Bruin winger Milan Lucic, who is called for the obvious trip.

Tanev and Alberts form a dependable defensive pairing. Vigneault and defence coach Rick Bowness make sure they don't overplay Alberts and Tanev, using them against Boston's third and fourth forward lines. After killing four penalties, the Canucks finally get a power play in the second, and another before the period is over. Vancouver has problems with the man advantages, however, as the Canuck centremen lose far too many faceoffs in the Boston zone. Tanev makes an incredibly accurate cross-ice pass in the second period, but Tanner Glass miscues on a glorious scoring opportunity near the Bruins goal, with Thomas caught above the crease, leaving an almost empty net. No shot, no goal and the game remains scoreless after forty minutes, with Canadian basketball great Steve Nash still encouraging fans by waving his white towel enthusiastically.

The revitalized Edler is credited with seven hits through two periods and eventually finishes in double digits with ten. He's more assertive with his play. Vigneault gets his way with line matchups, using Kesler against Patrice Bergeron and Lapierre versus David Krejci. Canuck fans are appreciative of their team's efforts, and also of heroes from days gone by. One-time captain Trevor Linden

A giant cut-out of Roberto Luongo decorates the top of a car arriving at Central City plaza in Surrey as coach Vigneault continues to go with the goalie that got him there. LES BAZSO/PNG

is spotted in the crowd and featured on the video replay screen, stirring a huge ovation for the leader of the 1994 Vancouver team that went to the final.

The tenacious Canucks are finally rewarded in the third when they score for the first time in six periods. Lapierre is the unlikely hero of Game 5 at 4:35 when he banks home a rebound off the end boards that hits Thomas and barely dribbles into the net. Bieksa purposely shoots wide on the play because his lane to the net is blocked by Lucic. The carom finds Lapierre at the far side of Thomas. Lapierre doesn't miss and leaps into the air in an emotional celebration. The Canucks clog the neutral zone for the rest of the game, using a passive forecheck in order to ensure the Bruins get no odd-man rushes. Vancouver plays with fire late in the game, however, when Malhotra loses three faceoffs in the Vancouver zone. The Canucks survive as Luongo stops ten shots in the third period and thirty-one overall for a 1-0 shutout, and retake the series lead at 3–2.

Canucks Nation is back on the bandwagon as fans shout "Luoooo, Luoooo," when Luongo is named first star. His best saves are on Bergeron (twice) in the first period as he posts his fourth shutout of these playoffs. Luongo makes sure he gives his stick to a fan, tossing it over the glass. Luongo has treated Game 5 against Boston the same as Game 7 against Chicago. He pulled on his hoodie after the morning skate and went for a relaxing walk along the seawall in Stanley Park. "I just focus on the journey and everything I need to do to be ready for the game, and that's what gets me prepared," says Luongo. "I try to block everything else out. Sometimes it's hard to do in a city like this."

On this night the city by the sea has another hero to celebrate in Lapierre, acquired at the trading deadline for depth. Lapierre has playoff experience with the Montreal Canadiens (thirty-five games over three years) and a knack for irritating the opposition. He's been a solid third-line centre with the Canucks, resilient and dependable, despite his antics like mocking Bergeron in the second game. "The third period, he was flying, skating with the puck," Burrows says about his fellow Quebecer. "I thought the Flower [Montreal great Guy Lafleur] was wearing No. 40 instead of No. 10. Growing up, watching our favourite team, Montreal, we had a lot of rivalries with the Boston Bruins. I don't know where it comes from, the hatred. But it's fun to play right now."

Lapierre is almost speechless after the game. He's still overcome with joy. "I didn't know what to do," he says. "So I just started jumping. It's been a long time [since scoring a big goal]. I just think I'm lucky to have that chance to come play for this team."

"He just happened to be in the right place at the right time," reasons Boston coach Claude Julien about the often wild-eyed Lapierre. The Canucks have the jump on the Bruins now, with Boston having plenty of think about during the 4,083 kilometre plane ride home for Game 6. For the Canucks, it's a much different journey. They are only a single victory from the franchise's first Stanley Cup championship.

## CHAPTER ELEVEN

*"We're going to keep taking punches because
that's the way we play."*
—Daniel Sedin after being roughed up
by Brad Marchand

The ventilation continues
in pumped-up Boston

The Canucks arrive in Boston to a raging controversy over what Roberto Luongo had to say about goaltending rival Tim Thomas after the fifth game. Luongo, in his post-game comments, mentions he would have made the save on the Maxim Lapierre goal because he plays much deeper in his crease than Thomas, a remark about Thomas's style that didn't go over well in the Bruins locker room. "It's not hard [to stop] if you're playing in the paint," Luongo points out. "It's an easy save for me, but if you're wandering out and aggressive like he is, that's going to happen."

The Lapierre goal, on a fortuitous bounce off the end boards from a wide point shot that went to the Vancouver player, was the first allowed by Thomas in 110 minutes and 42 seconds. Thomas has been Boston's best player in the final, his aggressive shot blocking spectacular. Luongo probably didn't mean to be critical with his off-the-cuff remark, but Thomas took it that way. Thomas has nothing to apologize for, of course, with his 1.21 goals-against average and .964 save percentage, both figures substantially superior to Luongo, especially after Boston's 8–1 drubbing of the Canucks in the third game.

If the Bruins need another rallying point, they've found one. But more importantly, the Boston players know they've done a better job than the Canucks in getting to the front of the net and playing with passion in the greasy areas. "I think it's part of the game that we have to play well," says Julien. "We need to get to the front of the net and win battles. If you're going to score goals, you have to win those battles. When you want to improve in certain areas, you bring that up in your practice. So it was meant for that reason."

Vigneault knows his team must play better on the road after dropping two lopsided games in Boston.

Canucks captain Henrik Sedin goes down hard in front of the Boston net. Canucks forwards couldn't penetrate the Bruins' punishing defense and when they did, goalie Thomas proved unbeatable. RIC ERNST/PNG/POSTMEDIA NEWS

He's hoping the Canucks feed off Luongo's shutout in Vancouver and can close the deal once and for all. The Canucks have a cushion in that they have two chances to win one game. "We all know we have to be better," states Vigneault. "We need to make every shift in every period count and that's what we're going to try to do."

Even though the Canucks have been outscored 12–1 in Boston, with second periods being their downfall, a huge entourage joins the team to Boston as the Canuck family gathers in anticipation of crowning a champion. Players have relatives from around North America and Europe fly in for Game 6. Aaron Rome is also with the team and makes his first public statement after his suspension, other than what was officially issued on his behalf after his season ended prematurely. He practises with the team because he wants to be part of the fabric. "It's a split-second decision and, if I could go back, I wish he didn't get hurt," Rome says. "But I don't think it would change my decision on the play. I've got to step up and be physical. That's part of my game and it's just unfortunate." If the Canucks win, Rome's name will be on the Stanley Cup because he played three games in the championship final.

Vigneault plans to dress the same lineup that played the fifth game. He still has concerns over the lack of production by the Sedins. They have combined for two points in total as the twins can't shake the tight checking of Chara and Seidenberg. The latter has stepped up brilliantly in the final series of the season. Winning is what matters most for the Sedins and the rest of the team, though, not individual points or plus-minus statistics. "Do you think in ten years anyone is going to remember who had the better plus-minus in the Stanley Cup final? Will people remember who had the better goals-against average?" Canuck defenceman Kevin Bieksa insists. "Of course not. They are just going to remember who won."

Moments before Game 6, the Bruins haul out one more legend when ninety-year-old Milt Schmidt (1936–55) is the official flag waver in the stands, cited as the "Ultimate Bruin." Schmidt and the Boston fans don't want a rival team to be awarded the Stanley Cup on their ice. There's been one constant in this series, other than the strong play of Thomas, in that the team that scores the first goal has won every game. That's why there's so much intensity as soon as the first puck is dropped at centre ice.

The Canucks suffer a blow early when left winger Mason Raymond is checked into the boards by Johnny Boychuk. No penalty is assessed by referees Dan O'Halloran and Kelly Sutherland, even though it's evident Boychuk has his stick between the legs of Raymond before pushing the Vancouver player into the boards. Raymond has no chance of keeping his balance when there's a stick between his legs. The tactic is called a can-opener and is considered highly illegal and dangerous, except by the officials in this instance. Raymond is helped from the ice and taken to hospital, where it's determined he has suffered a serious back injury. He may not return to hockey until the late fall at the earliest.

Boston gets the lead it so desperately wants courtesy of rookie Brad Marchand at 5:31 of the first period. The left winger cuts to the middle of the ice to take a pass and heads to the opposite wing before snapping a high shot to the short side over Luongo's catching glove. Thirty-five seconds later it's 2–0 when Milan Lucic beats

Luongo through the five-hole of his leg pads. Bieksa had dropped his stick in the corner and was late getting into position to defend Lucic.

The Canucks are reeling once again in Boston. The Bruins press hard on the gas pedal and go for the kill after a penalty to Edler for boarding. Boston defenceman Andrew Ference scores on a power play with a point shot after Malhotra loses another draw. Luongo is pulled after playing only eight minutes and thirty-five seconds. He's been crushed, beaten three times in eight shots. Schneider quickly gives up another goal when Michael Ryder defects a point shot by Tomas Kaberle. Boston has four goals in a span of four minutes and fourteen seconds. Game over.

The Canucks have been out-scored 16–1 during seven periods

Canucks speed merchant Mason Raymond, here shooting past Tomas Kaberle, left Game 6 with a fractured vertebrae after being tripped and pushed into the boards by Boston's Johnny Boychuk. Play went unpenalized. RIC ERNST/ PNG/POSTMEDIA NEWS

in Boston. Vancouver gets scoring chances, but can't beat Thomas. Julien has a belief that, when your team is physical, you can win games by three and four goals. He's absolutely right. Vigneault and the Canucks once again have no answer to the physicality of the Bruins at TD Garden. Vancouver scores twice in the meaningless final period, getting goals from Henrik Sedin on a power play and Lapierre sandwiched around a Boston marker by Mark Recchi on a two-man advantage. The Canucks power play is mostly discombobulated, with Thomas smothering everything so there are no second chances. In classic East versus West hockey, the physical East wins nearly every battle. No wonder the Bruins scored the four fastest goals in Cup final history.

Luongo tries to take the crushing defeat in stride after being jeered by ruthless Boston fans. "I have to believe in myself, right?" he says. "That's a big component of bouncing back and playing a good game." He talks about it being a dream to get to play in a Game 7 in the Stanley Cup final.

The "homer" series should favour the Canucks in the seventh and deciding game, but does it? They've played twenty-four games in sixty-one days and appear dead tired, beaten up physically and emotionally. The Bruins are the fresher team after winning Game 6 decisively. On top of that, most of the Canucks stood around and watched in the third period when the punkish Marchand fired a series of punches to the head of Daniel Sedin, who took the barrage without retaliation.

The spirit of the team is definitely in question. For the record, the Bruins have never participated in a Game 7 in the Stanley Cup final, though they won two series along the way this year in seventh games. The Canucks have a Cup final Game 7 under their belts, losing 3–2 in 1994 on the road to the New York Rangers. "I don't know why this is," sums up Bieksa, "but we go back to Vancouver where we're a different team."

## CHAPTER TWELVE

"This is absolutely the worst feeling of my career. It just feels terrible."
—Alex Edler as the long season ends

Canucks denied Cup as Vancouver burns

Storm clouds are gathering as Game 7 approaches in Vancouver. There is widespread worry about the Canucks, about Roberto Luongo, about the fragility of the entire team. Plus there's mounting concern over the huge crowds expected to converge on downtown streets at the end of the NHL playoffs. The city is ready to explode in celebration, but there's also trepidation that goes with a sporting event of this magnitude. What if the Canucks lose? They did in 1994 to the New York Rangers and riots ensued along trendy Robson Street. This time, a nervous city hopes there is better crowd control, with City Hall and police keeping fingers crossed, praying the Canucks provide the tonic that produces a peaceful salute to their springtime hockey heroes.

The theme for the deciding game is similar for both teams: it's one game and have no regrets. Don't leave anything on the ice. It's the twenty-fifth game of the post-season for each club, the marathon-like journey nearing an end. One Boston newspaper has called the performance of Luongo one of the greatest individual choke jobs in the history of the Stanley Cup final. That's hardly fair, considering Luongo has posted shutouts in two games in Vancouver, and won three times by a goal at Rogers Arena. Canuck players have Luongo's back by reassuring all who

Henrik Sedin battles Milan Lucic during the second period of Game 7. Boston had the answers when it came to shutting down the NHL's top scoring machine. RIC ERNST/PNG

choose to listen. "I've seen Lui have a lot of big bounce-back games," says Malhotra. "I don't see [the losses in Boston] changing our belief in him."

The Vancouver roster is paper-thin this late in the post-season, missing Raymond, Hamhuis and Samuelsson to injury. Others are hobbled, but play on. Raymond's Game 6 injury is diagnosed as a verte-brae compression fracture. Although he wasn't scoring, Raymond had provided speed on the attack and was re-liable killing penalties. "He's going to face a long, hard recovery," Canucks general manager Mike Gillis says about the next four months. "We've been told it's going to be very challenging for him and he's going to be in a difficult position for some time. I thought the Boston player [Johnny Boychuk] used a can-opener and drove him into the boards with enough force to break his back. That's what I saw." The NHL saw things differently, of course, with no penalty on the play and no suspension to follow.

What is the Vancouver strategy for Game 7? Vigneault plays his cards close to the vest, though it is speculated he'll use winger Tambellini in place of Raymond. Tambellini has the speed, but like Raymond, he really doesn't have the size to get by the rugged Bruins in the de-fensive zone. Almost forgotten in the tense atmosphere of the final is that Vigneault now has more play-off wins than any Vancouver NHL coach. The fifteen victories this year give him thirty-two, one more than Pat Quinn amassed. But with

OVERLEAF: Bewildered fan clutches his "Go Canucks" sign as mob violence rages around him following Vancouver's third Stanley Cup loss. ARLEN REDEKOP PHOTO/PNG

only eight goals in six games, the Canuck offence has Vigneault perplexed. Where does he turn for scoring?

Kesler and the Sedins have two goals combined through six games. Burrows and Lapierre have two each. Not one defenceman has scored a goal. "For us, injuries and adversity have been part of our daily routine throughout this season and we've faced every one of them head on," Vigneault says. "The guys that we have are going to jump on the opportunity. We worked all year long to get home ice, to play in front of these great fans, to feed off their energy."

The Bruins have a quiet confidence about them before the ultimate game of the season, especially goaltender Tim Thomas. "This is what every kid dreams about," says Thomas, thirty-seven, when his team gets to Vancouver. "The reality is, for me anyways, this may be the only Game 7 of the Stanley Cup final that I ever have in my career." Maybe Luongo is thinking the same thing. Luongo desperately wants to show he can win the biggest game on the NHL stage, just as he did internationally with the Canadian Olympic team in 2010 with an overtime win in the gold medal game in the same arena as this Game 7.

The 363rd consecutive sellout in Vancouver greets the Canucks for Game 7, with shouts of "We want the Cup!" beginning well before the national anthems. Tambellini is in the Vancouver lineup, replacing Raymond, and draws a punch from Boston captain Zdeno Chara after an early whistle. No penalty is assessed. Nothing has changed with the officiating. The crowd erupts into a huge ovation, not for a Luongo save, but when the video replay screen shows a shot of Raymond in street clothes

wearing a corset. Raymond smiles and waves assuredly. Meantime, huge crowds gather on the downtown streets, mostly along Georgia where they can view the game live on screens like the one outside the CBC studios.

Both teams hit hard and often. Burrows, Bieksa and Higgins are active for the Canucks early in the game, as are Lucic and Bergeron for the Bruins. Boston gets a strong forecheck from the fourth line of Shawn Thornton, Gregory Campbell and Daniel Paille. The Canucks don't have the same asset. The Bruins strike suddenly with that all-important first goal. Bergeron converts a cross-ice pass from Marchand after Salo is unable to contain Marchand on the cycle down low. Boston holds its 1-0 lead later in the opening period when Thomas makes a close-in stop on Tambellini after a rush with Kesler.

In the second, the Sedins frequently have possession

Luongo deflects a shot by Mark Recchi as time runs out on the Canucks in the third period of Game 7. MARK VAN MANEN/PNG

in the Boston zone, but end up feeding the points when they can't penetrate the Bruins' inner defence. Thomas plays his angles, blocking a dangerous shot by Kesler with his shoulder. There needs to be more net drive by the Canucks, but it doesn't materialize. Suddenly, Burrows is presented with a glorious scoring chance on a turnover, but it is Chara, slipping behind his goaltender, who prevents the tying goal.

The Bruins strike later in the second with two more goals, the first by the pesky Marchand as he skates behind the net before scoring from the side of the goal with a backhand shot. Bergeron adds insult to injury when he scores a shorthanded marker on a breakaway with Chara in the penalty box. Luongo seems confused when Bergeron slides into the net with the puck after being checked by chasing defenceman Ehrhoff. The goal counts, much to the chagrin of Luongo and Canucks fans. Boston has imposed its will on the reeling Canucks in the middle period, with Kesler about the only Vancouver player who is consistently a threat, using his speed through neutral ice to create space for scoring chances. Outside the rink on city streets, discontent brews among some of the estimated 100,000 fans without tickets.

The third period offers little hope for the Canucks. The Bruins play textbook defence-first hockey, giving up sixteen shots, mostly from long range. Vigneault juggles his lines, using Burrows with Kesler and putting Jannik Hansen with the Sedins. Nothing works for Vancouver as Boston defends tenaciously. Luongo is pulled for an extra attacker and that backfires when Marchand scores into an empty net. Thomas makes thirty-seven saves for his second shutout of the final and when the buzzer sounds he throws his stick and gloves into the air in celebration just before being mobbed by teammates. Boston has its first Stanley Cup championship in thirty-nine years. The Canucks remain Cup-less in forty NHL seasons.

Vancouver fans still chant "Go Canucks go!" as the teams proceed with the traditional handshakes. The Sedins show their class when they skate over to the on-ice officials and shake their hands, even after taking a terrible beating for seven games when the Bruins used seemingly illegal tactics. The Canucks raise their sticks in a salute to their loyal fan base before leaving the ice, mostly to cheers. Malhotra is the last to leave and is roundly applauded for his courageous comeback.

Most of the crowd stays for the post-game ceremonies. Fans boo NHL commissioner Gary Bettman when he walks up the red carpet to make a presentation. The jeers turn to cheers when Thomas is deservedly presented with the Conn Smythe Trophy as the most valuable player in the NHL playoffs. Chara is handed the Stanley Cup and holds it higher than it's ever been held by an NHL player before going for a brief skate, then passes the Cup to Mark Recchi, the oldest Boston player at forty-three. It's the third winning Cup team Recchi has played on. Later he announces his retirement.

Many fans wait patiently for another moment to express their appreciation for the efforts of a hometown boy. It happens five players after injured Nathan Horton is applauded, when the sixteenth Boston player raises the Cup. Milan Lucic, Vancouver-born and raised, has his moment, breaking into a huge grin almost as wide as that of captain Chara. "It's unbelievable," Lucic says.

"I guess it was meant to be." Just like it was in 2006, when he was with the junior Vancouver Giants and won the Memorial Cup on home ice at the Pacific Coliseum.

The mood in the Vancouver dressing room is solemn. Kesler talks about working eight years with the core members of the team for this chance, then failure. "To fall one game short, it's tough," he says. "It's probably the hardest thing I've ever done in my life. It's hard to swallow."

"Obviously we had something different in mind tonight," says Daniel Sedin. "I can't put into words how badly we feel." Henrik adds, "This is the best team I've been on by far. A lot of us have been here for a lot of years and we've grown up here and we've become a team here. We wanted to win for us foremost, but we wanted to win for the city as well." Canucks owner Francesco Aquilini expresses his feelings in the dim dressing room, saying how proud he is of his team, still unaware of what has amplified in the streets.

Outside Rogers Arena, disappointment turns into chaos. There is mayhem as malicious rioters burn cars and smash their way into stores to steal merchandise. The pride of the Canucks has turned into shame on the streets, with millions of dollars in damage. For all the good the Canucks have done by reaching their 107th game of the long season, it is blunted by an uncontrollable mob mentality outside their arena.

Vancouver fans give Milan Lucic a big hand, taking comfort from the fact that at least one born-and-bred Vancouver hockey player is getting to hoist the Stanley Cup.

MARK VAN MANEN/PNG

"It's such a great organization that you want to be here. I think everybody takes less to play here."

—Kevin Bieksa professing love for the
Vancouver hockey culture

A season with far more good than bad

The final numbers are in from the Stanley Cup final. It's a mixed bag at best. Daniel and Henrik Sedin, the celebrated twin brothers of the Canucks, are limited to a combined five points by the Boston Bruins in the seven-game series. Ryan Kesler, usually Vancouver's strongest skater, is held to a single assist, and that came in the first game. Mark Recchi and Brad Marchand each compiled seven points for the Bruins, who win the NHL playoff championship four games to three. Tim Thomas gets the shutout in Game 7, a 4–0 margin that caps off a scintillating series save percentage of .940 and confirms the Conn Smythe Trophy as the best player of the post-season.

The shame for the Canucks isn't so much that they were held to eight goals in losing to the Bruins, it's that they lost three times in Boston when outscored 17–3. Alain Vigneault was unable to squeeze another victory from his troops after the Canucks led the series 3–2 through five games. It's now eighteen years and counting since a Canadian team captured the Stanley Cup, with the Montreal Canadiens the last to earn the honour in 1993 with Patrick Roy in goal, John LeClair scoring overtime goals and Jacques Demers behind the bench.

The Canucks never trailed a

Nobody could deny 37-year-old Boston goalie Tim Thomas his moment in the sun after setting an NHL record for save percentage during the regular season and leading his team to the Stanley Cup with a dominating performance. RIC ERNST/PNG

series in the 2011 playoffs until the final was over. They experienced a season unlike no other Vancouver team, not even the one that went to Game 7 to the 1994 Cup final before losing 3–2 to the New York Rangers. This Canucks team became the first in franchise history to finish first overall in the standings, with 117 points, and earn the Presidents' Trophy and home ice advantage throughout the playoffs. Home ice helped when Vancouver won the seventh game in the opening series against the Chicago Blackhawks, eliminating the defending Cup champions. Unfortunately, playing at Rogers Arena in Game 7 against Boston didn't tip the scales. Boston simply was the better team over seven games, wearing down the Canucks with piston-like persistence in the physical side of the game.

While hooligans outside the arena tarnished the image of the City of Vancouver, the Canucks managed to increase the value of the franchise with their consistency through eighty-two regular-season games and another twenty-five in playoffs. They had the league scoring champion in Daniel Sedin and the top goaltending duo in Roberto Luongo and rookie Cory Schneider. They got fifty points from rushing defenceman Christian Ehrhoff and a bounce-back season from defender Kevin Bieksa, plus a forty-one-goal output from rising star Kesler.

In the end, though, the Canucks didn't have an answer to the physicality of the Bruins as Boston made life miserable for Vancouver's stars. The Canucks have nothing to apologize for because they left everything they had on the ice; they just didn't have anything more to offer. The tank was empty after seven games against Chicago, six against the Nashville Predators, five versus the San

Vancouver mayor Gregor Robertson adds own message to the wall of hope that appeared on boarded-up buidings the morning after the riot.

IAN SMITH/PNG

Jose Sharks and seven more against a Boston team that took great delight in administering a humbling beat-down. "We're devastated, but we're a good team and we'll be back," Luongo says after the season is over. "To fall short like that is a tough one to take. Playoffs is the hardest thing that I've ever had to do."

The Canucks and their loyal fans have plenty to be thankful for in the post-season. They saw Alex Burrows score in overtime to win Game 7 against Chicago. They saw a lucky bounce that allowed Bieksa to score in double overtime to eliminate San Jose. And, so memorably, they witnessed Manny Malhotra return in the final series after missing nearly three months following delicate eye surgery. General manager Mike Gillis puts things in perspective following the Boston series when he notes the Cup final wasn't reflective of the season's work by the Canucks. "It was a war of attrition," Gillis says of the final. "It's not an excuse. The better team on the ice won the series. We're going to make sure we continue to build depth that is playoff hockey depth, and retain our core players and try to replicate exactly what we did for 98 percent of this season."

This has been no ordinary hockey season in a hockey-crazed environment. Now the thoughtful Gillis has his work cut out because keeping teams together is a difficult task when there's free agency and a salary cap. Gillis wants to maintain skill level while adding missing pieces, perhaps a couple players with more pushback for when the Canucks play teams like Boston in the future. Part of the learning curve for the Canucks, he agrees, is competing with more resolve so they can reach their final goal.

There's some consolation when various Canucks are recognized at the NHL's annual awards ceremony in Las Vegas. Kesler takes home the Frank J. Selke Trophy as the forward who best excels at the defensive aspects of the game; Daniel Sedin gets the Art Ross Trophy for the scoring championship and the prestigious Ted Lindsay Award that goes to the league's most outstanding player as voted by fellow NHLers; Luongo and Schneider share the Jennings Trophy for allowing the least goals and Gillis is named General Manager of the Year.

Vigneault is a finalist for coach of the year, but loses to Dan Bylsma of the Pittsburgh Penguins, whose team was eliminated in the first round of the playoffs. Daniel Sedin does not win the Hart Trophy, with the MVP award voted by media going to Corey Perry of the Anaheim Ducks. Daniel and Henrik Sedin finish behind Dustin Brown of the Los Angeles Kings in voting for the NHL Foundation Award for contributions off the ice, while Luongo finishes back of Thomas in voting for the Vezina Trophy to the top individual goalkeeper.

Daniel Sedin tries to put the entire season in perspective when he suggests during the festivities in Las Vegas that everyone should be proud of the players and that there will be good Vancouver teams going forward. The players now have virtually every other acknowledgement, which leaves the single biggest prize after the Presidents' Trophy still to be hoisted by the Canucks. Thus, the fortieth season will long be remembered as the one that got away.

OVERLEAF: Thanks for the memories—and just wait until next season.

MARK VAN MANEN/PNG

211

#	PLAYER	GP	G	A	
22	Daniel Sedin	82	41	63	
33	Henrik Sedin	82	19	75	
17	Ryan Kesler	82	41	32	
26	Mikael Samuelsson	75	18	32	
5	Christian Ehrhoff	79	14	36	
14	Alexandre Burrows	72	26	22	
21	Mason Raymond	70	15	24	
23	Alexander Edler	51	8	25	
27	Manny Malhotra	72	11	19	
13	Raffi Torres	80	14	15	
36	Jannik Hansen	82	9	20	
2	Dan Hamhuis	64	6	17	
3	Kevin Bieksa	66	6	16	
10	Jeff Tambellini	62	9	8	
15	Tanner Glass	73	3	7	
6	Sami Salo	27	3	4	
41	Andrew Alberts	42	1	6	
4	Keith Ballard	65	2	5	
20	Chris Higgins	14	2	3	
29	Aaron Rome	56	1	4	
49	Alexandre Bolduc	24	2	2	
38	Victor Oreskovich	16	0	3	
18	Peter Schaefer	16	1	1	
57	Lee Sweatt	3	1	1	
39	Cody Hodgson	8	1	1	
54	Aaron Volpatti	15	1	1	
40	Maxim Lapierre	19	1	0	
37	Rick Rypien	9	0	1	
62	Mario Bliznak	4	1	0	
25	Sergei Shirokov	2	1	0	
18	Christopher Tanev	29	0	1	
24	Jonas Andersson	4	0	0	
32	Joel Perrault	7	0	0	
34	Guillaume Desbiens	12	0	0	
20	Ryan Parent	4	0	0	

= Player Number • GP = Games Played • G = Goals • A = Assists

	P	+/-	PIM	PP	SH	GW	S	S%
	104	30	32	18	0	10	266	15.4
	94	26	40	8	0	4	157	12.1
	73	24	66	15	3	7	260	15.8
	50	8	36	5	0	2	215	8.4
	50	19	52	6	0	3	209	6.7
	48	26	77	1	1	4	152	17.1
	39	8	10	2	1	5	197	7.6
	33	13	24	5	0	1	121	6.6
	30	9	22	3	1	2	111	9.9
	29	4	78	3	0	4	115	12.2
	29	13	32	0	0	2	113	8
	23	29	34	2	0	1	109	5.5
	22	32	73	1	0	2	105	5.7
	17	10	18	1	0	0	114	7.9
	10	-5	72	0	0	1	45	6.7
	7	-3	14	1	0	0	39	7.7
	7	0	41	0	0	0	21	4.8
	7	10	53	0	0	0	53	3.8
	5	0	6	1	0	0	34	5.9
	5	1	53	0	0	0	50	2
	4	1	21	0	0	1	21	9.5
	3	1	8	0	0	0	19	0
	2	-3	2	0	0	0	10	10
	2	4	2	0	0	1	4	25
	2	1	0	0	0	0	9	11.1
	2	-1	16	0	0	0	6	16.7
	1	-1	8	0	0	0	23	4.3
	1	-5	31	0	0	0	6	0
	1	1	0	0	0	0	1	100
	1	1	0	0	0	0	6	16.7
	1	0	0	0	0	0	15	0
	0	1	0	0	0	0	1	0
	0	-1	0	0	0	0	3	0
	0	-3	10	0	0	0	4	0
	0	-3	0	0	0	0	3	0

P = Points • +/- = Plus/Minus • PIM = Penalty Minutes • PP = Power Play Goals • SH = Short Handed Goals • GW = Game Winning Goals • S = Total Shots • S% = Shooting Percentage

#	PLAYER	GP	G	A	
47	Yann Sauve	5	0	0	
64	Evan Oberg	2	0	0	

#	GOALIE	GPI	GS	MIN	GAA	
1	Roberto Luongo	60	60	3590	2.11	
35	Cory Schneider	25	22	1372	2.23	

CANUCKS PLAYOFF SEASON STATISTICS

#	POS	PLAYER	GP	G	A	P	
33	C	Henrik Sedin	25	3	19	22	
22	L	Daniel Sedin	25	9	11	20	
17	C	Ryan Kesler	25	7	12	19	
14	L	Alexandre Burrows	25	9	8	17	
5	D	Christian Ehrhoff	23	2	10	12	
23	D	Alexander Edler	25	2	9	11	
3	D	Kevin Bieksa	25	5	5	10	
36	R	Jannik Hansen	25	3	6	9	
20	L	Chris Higgins	25	4	4	8	
21	L	Mason Raymond	24	2	6	8	
13	L	Raffi Torres	23	3	4	7	
2	D	Dan Hamhuis	19	1	5	6	
6	D	Sami Salo	21	3	2	5	
40	C	Maxim Lapierre	25	3	2	5	
26	R	Mikael Samuelsson	11	1	2	3	
29	D	Aaron Rome	14	1	0	1	
39	C	Cody Hodgson	12	0	1	1	
27	C	Manny Malhotra	6	0	0	0	
41	D	Andrew Alberts	9	0	0	0	
4	D	Keith Ballard	10	0	0	0	
10	L	Jeff Tambellini	6	0	0	0	
49	C	Alexandre Bolduc	3	0	0	0	
15	L	Tanner Glass	20	0	0	0	
38	R	Victor Oreskovich	19	0	0	0	
18	D	Christopher Tanev	5	0	0	0	

#	GOALIE	GPI	GS	MIN	GAA	W	
1	Roberto Luongo	25	24	1427	2.56	15	
35	Cory Schneider	5	1	163	2.58	0	

# = Player Number • GP = Games Played • G = Goals • A = Assists • GPI = Games Played In Net •
GS = Games Started • MIN = Minutes On Ice • GAA = Goals Against Average • POS = Position
• P = Points

P	+/-	PIM	PP	SH	GW	S	S%
0	-2	0	0	0	0	6	0
0	0	0	0	0	0	1	0

W	L	OT	SO	SA	GA	SV%	A	PIM
38	15	7	4	1753	126	0.928	3	2
16	4	2	1	714	51	0.929	3	0

+/-	PIM	PP	SH	GW	S	S%
-11	16	2	0	1	46	6.5
-9	32	5	0	2	99	9.1
0	47	4	0	2	76	9.2
0	34	1	1	2	62	14.5
-13	16	1	0	0	50	4
-4	8	0	0	0	58	3.4
6	51	1	0	1	47	10.6
7	18	0	0	0	50	6
1	2	1	0	3	49	8.2
-1	6	0	0	0	57	3.5
2	28	0	0	1	20	15
5	6	1	0	0	26	3.8
-4	2	3	0	1	33	9.1
2	66	0	0	1	42	7.1
-4	8	0	0	1	20	5
3	37	0	0	0	10	10
-4	2	0	0	0	12	0
-1	0	0	0	0	6	0
-8	6	0	0	0	6	0
-4	6	0	0	0	12	0
-3	2	0	0	0	2	0
0	0	0	0	0	2	0
-5	18	0	0	0	7	0
-6	12	0	0	0	14	0
0	0	0	0	0	2	0

L	OT	SO	SA	GA	SV%	G	A	PIM
10	0	4	711	61	0.914	0	0	0
0	0	0	82	7	0.915	0	0	0

P = Points • +/- = Plus/Minus • PIM = Penalty Minutes • PP = Power Play Goals • SH = Short Handed Goals • GW = Game Winning Goals • S = Total Shots • S% = Shooting Percentage • W = Wins • L = Losses • OT = Overtime Goals • SO = Shutouts • SA = Shots Against • GA = Goals Against • SV% = Save Percentage • A = Assists

NHL REGULAR SEASON SCORING LEADERS, BY POINTS

RANK	PLAYER	TEAM	POS	GP	G	A	P	
1	Daniel Sedin	VAN	L	82	41	63	104	
2	Martin St Louis	TBL	R	82	31	68	99	
3	Corey Perry	ANA	R	82	50	48	98	
4	Henrik Sedin	VAN	C	82	19	75	94	
5	Steven Stamkos	TBL	C	82	45	46	91	
6	Jarome Iginla	CGY	R	82	43	43	86	
7	Alex Ovechkin	WSH	L	79	32	53	85	
8	Teemu Selanne	ANA	R	73	31	49	80	
9	Henrik Zetterberg	DET	L	80	24	56	80	
10	Brad Richards	DAL	C	72	28	49	77	
11	Eric Staal	CAR	C	81	33	43	76	
12	Jonathan Toews	CHI	C	80	32	44	76	
13	Claude Giroux	PHI	R	82	25	51	76	
14	Ryan Getzlaf	ANA	C	67	19	57	76	
15	Ryan Kesler	VAN	C	82	41	32	73	
16	Patrick Marleau	SJS	L	82	37	36	73	
17	Thomas Vanek	BUF	L	80	32	41	73	
18	Patrick Kane	CHI	R	73	27	46	73	
19	Loui Eriksson	DAL	L	79	27	46	73	
20	Anze Kopitar	LAK	C	75	25	48	73	
21	Bobby Ryan	ANA	R	82	34	37	71	
22	Patrick Sharp	CHI	C	74	34	37	71	
23	Mike Ribeiro	DAL	C	82	19	52	71	
24	Joe Thornton	SJS	C	80	21	49	70	
25	Alex Tanguay	CGY	L	79	22	47	69	
26	Danny Briere	PHI	R	77	34	34	68	
27	Lubomir Visnovsky	ANA	D	81	18	50	68	
28	John Tavares	NYI	C	79	29	38	67	
29	Matt Duchene	COL	C	80	27	40	67	
30	Jeff Carter	PHI	C	80	36	30	66	

POS = Position • GP = Games Played • G = Goals • A = Assists • P = Points

+/-	ESP	SHP	PPP	HmP	RdP	DvP	ODvP	P/G
30	62	0	42	47	57	29	75	1.27
0	58	0	41	52	47	28	71	1.21
9	62	5	31	47	51	32	66	1.2
26	59	0	35	46	48	26	68	1.15
3	55	0	36	52	39	25	66	1.11
0	56	0	30	44	42	25	61	1.05
24	61	0	24	43	42	29	56	1.08
6	46	0	34	43	37	16	64	1.1
-1	49	1	30	41	39	16	64	1
1	48	0	29	45	32	21	56	1.07
-10	44	3	29	43	33	21	55	0.94
25	49	2	25	36	40	23	53	0.95
20	50	7	19	42	34	24	52	0.93
14	49	0	27	39	37	26	50	1.13
24	39	4	30	40	33	25	48	0.89
-3	44	3	26	49	24	27	46	0.89
2	45	0	28	40	33	22	51	0.91
7	49	0	24	33	40	23	50	1
10	45	3	25	39	34	21	52	0.92
25	54	1	18	37	36	17	56	0.97
15	60	1	10	44	27	24	47	0.87
-1	42	3	26	38	33	24	47	0.96
-4	48	0	23	36	35	20	51	0.87
4	35	2	33	42	28	21	49	0.88
0	49	0	20	41	28	21	48	0.87
20	53	0	15	26	42	16	52	0.88
18	37	0	31	41	27	20	48	0.84
-16	43	0	24	35	32	17	50	0.85
-8	52	0	15	33	34	19	48	0.84
27	49	0	17	33	33	19	47	0.82

+/- = Plus/Minus • ESP = Even Strength Points • SHP = Short Handed Points • PPP = Power Play Points • HmP = Home Points • RdP = Road Points • DvP = Division Points • ODvP = Other Division Points •P/G = Points Average Per Game

NHL PLAYOFF STATISTICS

RANK	PLAYER	TEAM	POS	GP	G	A	P
1	David Krejci	BOS	C	25	12	11	23
2	Henrik Sedin	VAN	C	25	3	19	22
3	Martin St Louis	TBL	R	18	10	10	20
4	Daniel Sedin	VAN	L	25	9	11	20
5	Patrice Bergeron	BOS	C	23	6	14	20
6	Brad Marchand	BOS	C	25	11	8	19
7	Ryan Kesler	VAN	C	25	7	12	19
8	Vincent Lecavalier	TBL	C	18	6	13	19
9	Alexandre Burrows	VAN	L	25	9	8	17
10	Nathan Horton	BOS	R	21	8	9	17
11	Michael Ryder	BOS	R	25	8	9	17
12	Teddy Purcell	TBL	R	18	6	11	17
13	Joe Thornton	SJS	C	18	3	14	17
14	Dan Boyle	SJS	D	18	4	12	16
15	Ryane Clowe	SJS	L	17	6	9	15
16	Pavel Datsyuk	DET	C	11	4	11	15
17	Logan Couture	SJS	C	18	7	7	14
18	Mark Recchi	BOS	R	25	5	9	14
19	Steve Downie	TBL	R	17	2	12	14
20	Patrick Marleau	SJS	L	18	7	6	13
21	Joel Ward	NSH	R	12	7	6	13
22	Steven Stamkos	TBL	C	18	6	7	13
23	Chris Kelly	BOS	C	25	5	8	13
24	Milan Lucic	BOS	L	25	5	7	12
25	Simon Gagne	TBL	L	15	5	7	12
26	Rich Peverley	BOS	C	25	4	8	12
27	Christian Ehrhoff	VAN	D	23	2	10	12
28	Claude Giroux	PHI	R	11	1	11	12
29	Sean Bergenheim	TBL	L	16	9	2	11
30	Dominic Moore	TBL	C	18	3	8	11

POS = Position • GP = Games Played • G = Goals • A = Assists • P = Points

+/-	PIM	PP	SH	GW	OT	S	S%	TOI/G	Sft/G	FO%
8	10	2	0	4	1	57	21.1	20:07	24.3	51.8
-11	16	2	0	1	0	46	6.5	20:56	29.6	45.8
-8	4	4	0	1	0	50	20	21:11	25	16.7
-9	32	5	0	2	0	99	9.1	20:12	28.6	25
15	28	0	2	1	0	67	9	18:42	28.8	60.2
12	40	0	1	1	0	61	18	16:46	24.1	28.6
0	47	4	0	2	1	76	9.2	22:34	30.6	54.1
6	16	3	0	3	1	56	10.7	19:51	24.7	49.9
0	34	1	1	2	2	62	14.5	20:40	31.1	50
11	35	1	0	3	2	52	15.4	16:54	21.9	33.3
8	8	2	0	2	1	44	18.2	14:34	19.3	0
4	2	1	0	1	0	46	13	13:42	19.4	18.2
-5	16	0	0	2	1	48	6.3	22:15	31.4	59.2
-7	8	2	0	1	0	67	6	26:10	31.1	0
5	32	3	0	0	0	39	15.4	19:27	26.3	33.3
10	8	2	0	0	0	38	10.5	21:09	28.7	55.2
2	2	1	0	0	0	64	10.9	19:23	28.8	45.2
7	8	2	0	1	0	40	12.5	16:09	22.5	47.4
7	40	0	0	1	0	27	7.4	12:35	17.4	47.8
-1	9	3	0	1	0	59	11.9	22:21	31.2	47.2
4	6	2	0	1	0	28	25	20:25	29.5	39.5
-5	6	3	0	1	0	46	13	19:43	24	50.8
11	6	0	0	0	0	28	17.9	15:28	23	47.9
11	63	1	0	0	0	56	8.9	17:54	22.7	21.4
6	4	0	0	1	0	21	23.8	15:52	21.5	75
6	17	0	0	2	0	42	9.5	16:11	23.2	53.5
-13	16	1	0	0	0	50	4	22:26	28.6	0
2	8	0	0	0	0	21	4.8	21:57	28.6	55.7
2	8	0	0	1	0	46	19.6	14:09	21.1	47.4
-3	18	1	0	0	0	26	11.5	17:46	24.8	48.4

+/- = Plus/Minus • PIM = Penalty In Minutes • PP = Power Play Goals • SH = Short Handed Goals • GW = Game Winning Goals • OT = Overtime Goals • S = Total Shots • S% = Shooting Percentage • TOI/G = Time On Ice Per Game • Sft/G = Average Shifts Per Game • FO% = Faceoff Win Percentage

NHL REGULAR SEASON LEAGUE STANDINGS – EASTERN DIVISIO

RANK	TEAM	DIV	GP	W	L	OT	P	ROW	
1	Z - Washington	SE	82	48	23	11	107	43	
2	Y - Philadelphia	ATL	82	47	23	12	106	44	
3	Y - Boston	NE	82	46	25	11	103	44	
4	X - Pittsburgh	ATL	82	49	25	8	106	39	
5	X - Tampa Bay	SE	82	46	25	11	103	40	
6	X - Montréal	NE	82	44	30	8	96	41	
7	X - Buffalo	NE	82	43	29	10	96	38	
8	X - Ny Rangers	ATL	82	44	33	5	93	35	
9	Carolina	SE	82	40	31	11	91	35	
10	Toronto	NE	82	37	34	11	85	32	
11	New Jersey	ATL	82	38	39	5	81	35	
12	Atlanta	SE	82	34	36	12	80	29	
13	Ottawa	NE	82	32	40	10	74	30	
14	Ny Islanders	ATL	82	30	39	13	73	26	
15	Florida	SE	82	30	40	12	72	26	

NHL REGULAR SEASON LEAGUE STANDINGS – WESTERN DIVISIO

RANK	TEAM	DIV	GP	W	L	OT	P	ROW	
1	P - Vancouver	NW	82	54	19	9	117	50	
2	Y - San Jose	PAC	82	48	25	9	105	43	
3	Y - Detroit	CEN	82	47	25	10	104	43	
4	X - Anaheim	PAC	82	47	30	5	99	43	
5	X - Nashville	CEN	82	44	27	11	99	38	
6	X - Phoenix	PAC	82	43	26	13	99	38	
7	X - Los Angeles	PAC	82	46	30	6	98	36	
8	X - Chicago	CEN	82	44	29	9	97	38	
9	Dallas	PAC	82	42	29	11	95	37	
10	Calgary	NW	82	41	29	12	94	32	
11	St Louis	CEN	82	38	33	11	87	34	
12	Minnesota	NW	82	39	35	8	86	36	
13	Columbus	CEN	82	34	35	13	81	29	
14	Colorado	NW	82	30	44	8	68	24	
15	Edmonton	NW	82	25	45	12	62	23	

DIV = Division • GP = Games Played • W = Wins • L = Losses • OT = Overtime Goals • P = Points
• ROW = Regulation plus Overtime Wins

GF	GA	DIFF	HOME	AWAY	SO	L10	STREAK
224	197	27	25-8-8	23-15-3	5-6	7-2-1	LOST 1
259	223	36	22-12-7	25-11-5	3-7	3-4-3	WON 1
246	195	51	22-13-6	24-12-5	2-6	6-3-1	LOST 1
238	199	39	25-14-2	24-11-6	10-3	8-2-0	WON 4
247	240	7	25-11-5	21-14-6	6-6	7-3-0	WON 2
216	209	7	24-11-6	20-19-2	3-3	5-4-1	WON 1
245	229	16	21-16-4	22-13-6	5-1	8-1-1	WON 4
233	198	35	20-17-4	24-16-1	9-3	6-3-1	WON 1
236	239	-3	22-14-5	18-17-6	5-5	7-2-1	LOST 1
218	251	-33	18-15-8	19-19-3	5-6	6-3-1	LOST 2
174	209	-35	22-16-3	16-23-2	3-2	4-5-1	WON 1
223	269	-46	17-17-7	17-19-5	5-7	4-6-0	LOST 2
192	250	-58	16-20-5	16-20-5	2-5	5-4-1	LOST 1
229	264	-35	17-18-6	13-21-7	4-6	3-6-1	LOST 1
195	229	-34	16-17-8	14-23-4	4-7	1-7-2	WON 1

GF	GA	DIFF	HOME	AWAY	SO	L10	STREAK
262	185	77	27-9-5	27-10-4	4-5	7-3-0	WON 2
248	213	35	25-11-5	23-14-4	5-5	7-2-1	WON 1
261	241	20	21-14-6	26-11-4	4-4	4-4-2	WON 1
239	235	4	26-13-2	21-17-3	4-2	7-3-0	WON 3
219	194	25	24-9-8	20-18-3	6-4	7-2-1	LOST 1
231	226	5	21-13-7	22-13-6	5-6	5-3-2	LOST 1
219	198	21	25-13-3	21-17-3	10-2	6-4-0	LOST 2
258	225	33	24-17-0	20-12-9	6-5	5-4-1	LOST 1
227	233	-6	22-11-8	20-18-3	5-7	4-4-2	LOST 1
250	237	13	23-13-5	18-16-7	9-7	5-2-3	OT 1
240	234	6	23-13-5	15-20-6	4-6	6-2-2	WON 1
206	233	-27	19-17-5	20-18-3	3-5	4-6-0	WON 2
215	258	-43	17-19-5	17-16-8	5-8	1-6-3	LOST 4
227	288	-61	16-21-4	14-23-4	6-1	2-8-0	WON 1
193	269	-76	13-22-6	12-23-6	2-9	2-6-2	OT 1

GF = Goals For • GA = Goals Against • DIFF = Goal Differential • SO = Shutouts • L10 = Record in Last 10 Games

CANUCKS TEAM ROSTER

#	PLAYER	POS	BIRTH DATE	BIRTH PLACE	HT	WT
1	Roberto Luongo	G	4-Apr-79	Montreal, QC	6'3"	208
2	Dan Hamhuis	D	13-Dec-82	Smithers, BC	6'0"	209
3	Kevin Bieksa	D	16-Jun-81	Grimsby, ON	6'0"	198
4	Keith Ballard	D	26-Nov-82	Baudette, MN, USA	5'11"	208
5	Christian Ehrhoff	D	6-Jul-82	Moers, GER	6'2"	203
6	Sami Salo	D	2-Sep-74	Turku, FIN	6'3"	212
10	Jeff Tambellini	LW	13-Apr-84	Calgary, AB	5'11"	186
13	Raffi Torres	LW	8-Oct-81	Toronto, ON	6'0"	216
14	Alexandre Burrows	LW	11-Apr-81	Pincourt, QC	6'1"	199
15	Tanner Glass	LW	29-Nov-83	Regina, SK	6'1"	210
17	Ryan Kesler	C	31-Aug-84	Livonia, MI, USA	6'2"	202
18	Peter Schaefer	LW	12-Jul-77	Yellow Grass, SK	6'1"	200
18	Chris Tanev	D	20-Dec-89	Toronto, ON	6'2"	199
20	Chris Higgins	C	2-Jun-83	Smithtown, NY, USA	6'0"	205
20	Ryan Parent	D	17-Mar-87	Prince Albert, SK	6'3"	198
21	Mason Raymond	LW	17-Sep-85	Cochrane, AB	6'0"	185
22	Daniel Sedin	LW	26-Sep-80	Ornskoldsvik, SWE	6'1"	187
23	Alexander Edler	D	21-Apr-86	Ostersund, SWE	6'4"	215
24	Jonas Andersson	RW	24-Feb-81	Lidingö, SWE	6'3"	204
25	Sergei Shirokov	LW	10-Mar-86	Moscow, RUS	5'10"	195
26	Mikael Samuelsson	RW	23-Dec-76	Mariefred, SWE	6'1"	218
27	Manny Malhotra	C	18-May-80	Missisauga, ON	6'2"	208
29	Aaron Rome	D	27-Sep-83	Nesbitt, MB	6'1"	218
32	Joel Perrault	C	6-Apr-83	Montreal, QC	6'2"	212
33	Henrik Sedin	C	26-Sep-80	Ornskoldsvik, SWE	6'2"	188
34	Guillaume Desbiens	D	20-Apr-85	Alma, QC	6'3"	216
35	Cory Schneider	G	18-Mar-86	Marblehead, MA, USA	6'2"	195
36	Jannik Hansen	LW	15-Mar-86	Herlev, DNK	6'1"	195
37	Rick Rypien	C	16-May-84	Blairmore, AB	5'11"	190
38	Victor Oreskovich	D	15-Aug-86	Whitby, ON	6'3"	215
39	Cody Hodgson	C	18-Feb-90	Toronto, ON	6'0"	185
40	Maxim Lapierre	C	29-Mar-85	Saint-Léonard, QC	6'2"	207
41	Andrew Alberts	D	30-Jun-81	Minneapolis, MN, USA	6'5"	209
47	Yann Sauve	D	18-Feb-90	Montreal, QC	6'3"	209
49	Alexandre Bolduc	C	26-Jun-85	Montreal, QC	6'3"	200
54	Aaron Volpatti	RW	30-May-85	Revelstone, BC	6'0"	215
57	Lee Sweatt	D	13-Aug-85	Elburn, IL, USA	5'9"	195
62	Mario Bliznak	C	6-Mar-87	Trencin, SVK	6'0"	185
64	Evan Oberg	D	16-Feb-88	Forestburg, AB	6'0"	165

Index